KEY STAGE 2:

HELPING WITH READING DIFFICULTIES

by

JANE CALVER

SANDY RANSON

DOROTHY SMITH

A NASEN Publication

Published in 1999

ISBN 1 901485 05 6

Published by NASEN.
NASEN is a registered charity. Charity No. 1007023.
NASEN is a company limited by guarantee, registered in England and Wales.
Company No. 2674379.

Further copies of this book and details of NASEN's many other publications may be obtained from the NASEN Bookshop at its registered office:
NASEN House, 4/5, Amber Business Village, Amber Close, Amington, Tamworth, Staffs., B77 4RP.
Tel: 01827 311500 Fax: 01827 313005; email: welcome@nasen.org.uk

Copy editing by Nicola von Schreiber.
Cover design by Raphael Creative Design.
Typeset by J. C. Typesetting.
Typeset in Times and printed in the United Kingdom by Stowes (Stoke-on-Trent).

KEY STAGE 2:
HELPING WITH READING DIFFICULTIES

Contents

Acknowledgements

The authors would like to thank Mike Hinson and Alec Williams of NASEN's Publications Sub-committee for their helpful comments and advice.

The extract on page 17 from *Fantastic Mr. Fox* by Roald Dahl is reproduced with the permission of the publishers, David Higham Associates, 5-8 Lower John Street, Golden Square, London W1R 4HA.

Foreword

Aims

Young readers of today are tomorrow's parents and teachers. We, as educators, have a duty to make reading as pleasurable and as exciting a task as possible as well as being an effective tool which will enable the individual to cope effectively with modern-day living.

Reading is a complex skill linking visual and phonological tasks in order to provide meaning from words and texts. Some pupils enter school already able to read, others learn to read with little difficulty whilst others struggle throughout their school lives. Reading is fundamental to learning and without this skill pupils become disadvantaged, as the foreword to *The National Literacy Strategy* (DfEE, 1998) stresses. The 80 per cent target of 11-year-olds achieving the standard of literacy for their age by the year 2002 is an ambitious one. Already there are literacy summer schools to help borderline pupils catch up. *The National Literacy Strategy* presents targets and teaching objectives for each year group and by Year 6 it is expected that competent readers will be able to discuss reading materials of different genres and to comprehend readily the texts they are reading.

But what of the remaining 20 per cent and in particular the 18 per cent or so of pupils who are taught in mainstream education? *The National Literacy Strategy* framework includes them but as yet does not truly cater for them.

There are many books about the teaching of reading, both practical and theoretical. There are many books about reading problems which cover the whole age-range but little is written about the weak or reluctant reader in Key Stage 2. This book will address that fact as it aims to give practical advice to the many teachers who are concerned about pupils who have reading problems within their classes.

The idea for this book arose from a set of in-service sessions delivered by the authors. The sessions dealt with a general introduction to reading and particular reading difficulties at Key Stage 2, assessment techniques and ideas for helping with phonic, visual and language strategies, and concluded with a discussion about motivational aspects.

Issues addressed later

The initial section attempts to place reading within the context of the school and to discuss briefly the processes of reading both within the pupil and within the text. Part 1 of this book investigates easy-to-apply identification and assessment strategies which can be carried out within the context of the classroom. Part 2 explores the different strategies which can be used for the teaching of reading which will fit what has been discovered about the particular pupil's strengths and weaknesses. Although these are written in separate chapters (visual, auditory, language and motivational areas) the authors reiterate that reading and the teaching of reading needs all four working in conjunction as none stands alone. Part 3 discusses different organisational aspects, discusses working with parents and looks into the issues of resourcing. The organisation of *The National Literacy Strategy's* 'Literacy Hour' will be alluded to as here it is suggested that class teachers will have time within the structured framework to work intensively on structured and guided reading (and writing) activities with small groups of pupils. There may be instances where some pupils would find it difficult to cope within the expected whole class session on the type of literacy work prepared for Key Stage 2 pupils. Division of pupils into ability or attainment groups will also be discussed.

Education in Scotland and Northern Ireland does not use England's English National Curriculum. However, the former's English Language 5-14 and the Northern Ireland English Curriculum have similarities.

Setting the scene

Introduction

Fluent readers read swiftly and competently, internalising the print on the page and extracting meaning from it. Becoming a fluent reader is a complex affair. One of our main aims in education is that all pupils will be able to use books and other reading materials for a wide range of purposes and that they will be able to achieve this with pleasure rather than pain. Reading should not be merely functional but should be recreational and, therefore, enjoyable as well.

Reading past and present

The reading debate tended to be polarised into two distinct camps. One was the top down or 'real books' approach. Learners were thought to acquire reading by:

- being read to
- reading alongside the adult
- using the adult as a model in order to imitate reading
- reading, reading and more reading until the learner became a reader needing no prop or supporter.

The other was the 'bottom up' approach where:

- discrete skills were identified (e.g. use of phonics)
- these skills were taught often in isolation from the text
- these skills were taught in order and carefully consolidated and overlearned until the application of these skills produced readers who had the requisite tools for approaching the task in hand.

These two rather conflicting views had vociferous and passionate exponents. This whole debate has been superceded by *The National Literacy Strategy* which requires teachers to use an integrated approach to the teaching of reading.

The importance of reading policies

Ideally schools should have reading policies embedded within their English policies. These should stress the importance of reading within the school and the wider community. From this rationale aims and objectives are derived. Long-term aims would be those that strive for pupils leaving the primary sector to be as literate as possible and for pupils to enjoy the process of reading. In order to achieve these aims reference to teaching approaches should be included both for general class teaching and also for those pupils who find the acquisition of reading difficult. Teaching approaches may depend upon the school's resources; however, they should not be governed by these. Schools' reading resources need to be as wide and as varied as possible. Sometimes a school will spend a great deal of money on one particular scheme or approach only to find that this does not work well for its particular pupils. Before purchasing expensive resources, schools need to research and check their usefulness as carefully and as thoroughly as possible.

There should also be indications of the assessment and monitoring procedures within the school policy. *The National Literacy Strategy* is not introducing new assessment procedures but it indicates that regular assessment of progress and systematic recording procedures are important. Assessment is a very important part of the teaching of reading. There may be pupils working their way through reading schemes in early stages who can read quite fluently. Their reading is only checked through the completion of the books on the particular level and little wider reading takes place. This might make them bored with the reading process and lead them to dislike reading. It is necessary to guard against the over-supportive use of reading schemes where pupils are helped and encouraged through familiar texts but fail to develop independent strategies of their own.

The National Literacy Strategy also gives information about monitoring which is linked to teaching. It suggests that pupils are involved with their own learning by being made aware of *what* they are learning and *why* they are undertaking certain activities. This is an important point which is sometimes overlooked when pupils are taught on particular reading programmes.

There should be clear links between the Reading Policy and the Special Needs Policy of the school. Those pupils with reading difficulties might need to be placed on the staged process which is outlined in *The Code of Practice on the Identification and Assessment of Special Educational Needs* (DfE, 1994) and which has been adapted by many LEAs and schools to suit their own particular circumstances. *The National Literacy Strategy* discusses the use of Individual Education Plans (IEPs) for the setting of targets linked with the term's teaching objectives. It is important that pupils with reading difficulties are set achievable short-term targets which link to long-term goals. It is recognised that within different classes and different schools pupils with reading difficulties might be placed on any of the stages of *The Code*.

From Key Stage 1 to Key Stage 2

The majority of pupils in Key Stage 1 achieve a satisfactory standard in reading before transferring to Key Stage 2. The current reading targets of the National Curriculum are reached and the pupils are ready to progress to more complex areas of reading.

By the end of Key Stage 1 they are expected to be able to:

- read a range of texts fluently and accurately
- read independently with appropriate strategies which establish meaning
- read both fiction and non-fiction showing understanding of the main points
- express preferences
- use alphabetic knowledge to find books and information.

The National Literacy Strategy details high frequency words to be learnt by sight, a range of phonic knowledge to be used and the different types of reading material to be covered. By the end of the third term in Year 2 pupils should be well on their way to becoming fully literate.

However, there are those pupils who find reading very difficult; who for some reason or another have made little start to the process of reading. These pupils enter Key Stage 2 at a disadvantage for they are unable to use the written word to access the many aspects of the curriculum which are presented in books, magazines and in other forms of print. It is possible that Year 3 pupils may continue to cope with those same teaching methods that were used previously but what if they continue to 'fail'? 'Early Years' methods may not be suitable for older primary pupils even though these pupils still need to acquire early basic skills or consolidate these by constant repetitive practice.

The National Literacy Strategy acknowledges that younger readers in Key Stage 1 find reading familiar texts fairly easy because the stories are known, the story language is predictable and the vocabulary is repetitive. However, the reading demands of Key Stage 2 require decoding skills which need systematic teaching because of the complexities found in less common words. *The National Literacy Strategy* is quite prescriptive in that it sets out what pupils should be taught each term from Year R to Year 6 and it covers work at Text Level, Sentence Level and Word Level. It is cumulative and reinforcing. For example, Year 3 pupils in term one will be expected to use their knowledge of phonics as a cue when reading simple and unfamiliar texts. By the third term of Year 6 pupils will be expected to use 'fast and flexible' word attack skills which derive from phonic and word recognition knowledge alongside grammatical and contextual strategies when they read unfamiliar and 'challenging' texts. Word level skills which help to teach reading finish at the end of Year 4. There is much for the pupil with no literacy problems to assimilate. The pupil who has reading and other allied literacy difficulties will find the work even more demanding.

Reading as part of the English Curriculum
Reading is only one of the components of the English curriculum and as such is difficult to separate from speaking, listening, spelling and writing. It is recognised that *The National Literacy Strategy* does not separate reading from spelling nor do other books concerned with the acquisition of literacy. However, this book, although mentioning the relationship between the 'read' word and the 'spelt' word, will concentrate on the former.

Why some pupils have reading difficulties
There are many reasons why some pupils cannot read easily.

- Some have missed vital stages in their early years and because of this have not learnt those skills which are important for reading acquisition.
- Others have particular weaknesses in their cognitive abilities which make all areas of learning a slow and laborious process.
- Some show particular difficulties with oral language which add to their problems with written language acquisition.
- There are those who have particular problems with their hearing or sight. Hearing problems might delay auditory (phonic) approaches whilst visual problems might lead to difficulties with discrimination and tracking.
- Some pupils display inappropriate behaviours which prevent them from learning.
- Those pupils with specific learning difficulties (e.g. dyslexia) sometimes reach a plateau in their reading after a bank of known sight words are learnt as they do not have the phonological awareness or the ability to use the phonic structure of words in any helpful way. Conversely it may be that their visual memory is at fault so they slowly read by decoding into phonic components every word they meet, even trying to decode those words which appear to be irregular.
- There are pupils for whom English is an additional language who may find the process of learning to read difficult.
- Those pupils who for various reasons have very low confidence in their abilities sometimes cannot learn because of all-pervasive emotional problems.
- The pace of *The National Literacy Strategy* at Key Stage 1 may cause difficulties for some pupils. By Key Stage 2 they may not have acquired the necessary basic areas of skills and knowledge.
- The school or class may have been inadequately resourced. Most pupils need a variety of books and additional activities which are 'pupil-friendly' and exciting.

Teachers have such pupils in their classes. It would be hard to think that there are pupils entering school who are reluctant to learn to read and who do not enjoy the world of books in the same way as their peers. But by the time they reach Key Stage 2 and if they see themselves as failures, reading is not enjoyable and is only perceived as hard work. All pupils are entitled to be well supported and well taught. One cannot guarantee that all pupils will reach a reading level equivalent to their age level when they leave Key Stage 2. It is to be hoped that the vast majority of pupils will attain a functional reading level where they can cope with much of the reading material on offer except for those with the most entrenched problems.

There are two types of problem which might make reading difficult for pupils. One stems from within the pupil and the other from within the reading material.

Pupils may experience difficulties with the actual mechanics of reading because of:

- weak sight word recognition
- problems with phonic decoding
- difficulties with multi-syllabic word synthesising
- contextual cueing problems
- poor vocabulary understanding and usage which limit coping with the language of the text
- problems with visual and auditory memories, particularly the latter which might affect both long and short-term retention
- weaknesses with understanding and use of language
- problems with acquiring higher reading skills which might be out of their immediate understanding.

Within the work there can be problems with:

- the readability of the text
- the words used (the complexity of their meaning)
- the length of sentences
- the overall appearance of the books or reading material including the layout and print
- the complexity of some words which might inhibit ease of decoding (although some texts may be easy enough for memorising, especially if the content is made up of repetitive sentences)
- some non-fiction texts because of the specialised vocabulary and content.

What is needed in order to read

In order to be able to read without problems the learner needs:

- to perceive the need to read
- good vision
- good hearing
- adequate visual discrimination and memory skills
- adequate phonological awareness
- adequate auditory discrimination and auditory memory skills
- to be aware of book and story language
- to be competent with their own expressive language abilities
- to be competent at understanding vocabulary (received language)
- no emotional worries which might prevent learning
- no prior discouraging environmental circumstances or learning experiences.

The importance of learning all reading strategies

In order for reading to cover all the necessary strands no one strategy stands alone. Marilyn Jaegar Adams (1990) succinctly encapsulates all that is required for fluent reading.

> In both fluent reading and its acquisition the reader's knowledge must be aroused interactively and in parallel. Neither understanding nor learning can proceed hierarchically from the bottom up. Phonological awareness, letter recognition facility, familiarity with spelling patterns, spelling-sound relationships, and individual words must be developed in concert with real reading and real writing and with deliberate reflection of the forms, functions and meanings of texts.

6

Any one approach to teaching reading used in isolation will not help all pupils to become competent readers. The approach advocated within this book, in line with *The National Literacy Strategy*, emphasises the need for an integrated approach which draws together all the skills needed for reading.

The National Literacy Project talked of a set of 'searchlights', each shedding light on the text;

The aim of the successful reader is to use as many of these searchlights as possible. Each sheds a partial light and together, they make a mutually supporting system. The fewer the searchlights the reader can switch on, the more dependent he/she is on a single one. As pupils learn to read they need to be taught how to draw on all this knowledge and orchestrate it so that each searchlight or 'cue' is used to reinforce and check the others.

Reason and Boote (1994) also give a model of literacy learning in their publication *Helping Children with Reading and Spelling*. They explore and clarify the link between reading and writing and their model stresses the way that 'meaning' (the way the reader responds to print and the understanding that is brought to the written word in all its facets) and 'phonics' and 'fluency' (immediate word recognition) work together for ease of reading acquisition.

How pupils read

When pupils are read to and later when they read for themselves they use contextual strategies where meaning is provided by semantic and/or syntactic cues. They also use visual and phonic strategies.

- *Semantic cues* give the reader information about word definitions. (For example, a Year 6 girl read the word 'dispatch' using phonic decoding but was unable to gain meaning from this because this word was not in her vocabulary.)
- *Syntactic cues* rely on grammatical awareness. If pupils do not match subject and verb in speech it is doubtful that they will do so when reading. (For example, in speech a pupil might say 'The houses is red'.)
- *Visual strategies* enable the reader to use the printed letter string on the page to match a stored visual feature within the memory that corresponds to a known or familiar word. (Here homonyms have to be checked with semantic cueing in order to determine their pronunciation such as 'wind' or 'read'.)
- *Phonic awareness* and usage requires the reader to use knowledge of correspondences between letters and sounds to generate either full or partial phonological recoding. (For example, the word 'fog' is divided into its phonemes 'f-o-g' and blended to pronounce the word or the 'og' unit of rime might be recalled from 'dog' and the first phoneme then changed.) Within this strategy the learner starts with basic or rudimentary knowledge which gradually becomes more sophisticated especially when visual strategies help with analogies (e.g. when the reader knows 'night' and the 'ight' unit of sound then the word 'flight' can be attempted).

Readability of material in Key Stage 2

By the time the learner enters Key Stage 2 there are more and more instances where reading is required. Reading matter contains core words which are frequently repeated. These are the high frequency words which make up the bulk of reading material. Other, less common, words can be either learnt by heart, decoded through some type of phonic or multi-syllabic synthesis or can be guessed at through contextual clueing.

There are, of course, readability formulae which can be applied but these tend to fix on a reading level rather than to analyse carefully the actual words used. Formulae such as the Fog Index and graphs such as Fry examine the length of sentences and length of multi-syllabic words in passages of 100 words. In this way a calculation is obtained which gives the book a readability level. What formulae such as these cannot do is to look at the attractiveness of the books, their layout, the clarity of the print on the page, the illustrations and the subject matter. Pupils can be quite adept at finding books which suit them. Both interest age and readability level need to be taken into account especially at Key Stage 2 where pupils may have low reading ages but quite sophisticated interests. The publication *The NASEN A to Z: A Graded List of Reading Books* (Hinson & Gains, 1997) is a resource guide to help teachers to match the individual needs of readers with reading scheme materials. There are also computer programs which work out the readability calculations. However, if reading levels are worked out using the computer, one still has to type the relevant numbers of words in order for the calculation to take place. Most readability formulae are based on North American school grade levels and this has to be taken into account.

The Basic Skills Agency produces a *SMOG Ready Reckoner* on a pocket-sized card which gives a seven-point set of instructions for working out the readability level of books. This is based on the number of words having three and more syllables and is quick to use and easy to understand.

Another way to check the suitability of reading books is to select a section of 100 words from the text and compare this against a list of high frequency words (e.g. from *The National Literacy Strategy*). Irregular words which cannot be easily decoded should be listed separately (such as 'people' or 'water'). Words that can be decoded can then be subdivided into two groups of regular words. The first group of words comprise those which contain short vowels, initial consonants, consonant digraphs and blends and common units of sound (e.g. 'all', 'end', 'amp' and 'ing'). The second group comprise words with more complicated phonic units and words of more than one syllable. (*The National Literacy Strategy* gives a suggested order for teaching phonics which could prove helpful in this respect.) From these lists a percentage for each section can be made. (See the appendix for more examples, pages 58-60.)

PART 1
Identification and assessment strategies

Why assess?
At the heart of every school and every class lies a cycle of planning, teaching and assessing.

(Code of Practice para. 2:1, DfE, 1994)

As teachers we are increasingly required to assess pupils' progress in a variety of ways. The National Curriculum Levels attained by pupils need to be assessed by teachers in the light of the level descriptions within each curriculum document – these judgements are supplemented by the end of Key Stage tests and tasks. However, there is increasing awareness that the assessment and monitoring of progress needs to be ongoing and is not an exercise which is confined to the end of each Key Stage. How else, other than by thorough assessment, can vital questions about the rates of progress, quality of learning, effectiveness of teaching, and suitability of methods and materials etc. be answered?

The Code provides a useful model for the assessment and planning for individual need. It is suggested that the pupil's teacher will:

- gather information about the pupil and make an initial assessment of the pupil's special educational needs
- provide special help within the normal curriculum framework, exploring ways in which increased differentiation of classroom work might better meet the needs of the individual pupil
- monitor and review the pupil's progress.

(para. 2.73)

Assessment as part of school policy
Whilst such a model may well apply to other curriculum areas, one should consider its usefulness when assessing pupils' reading difficulties. As has already been discussed in the opening chapter of this book, there is a multiplicity of reasons why a pupil might be experiencing reading difficulties. Indeed a number of factors may be contributory. Some reading difficulties may prove deep seated and in such a case are likely to indicate that a pupil has special educational needs. This book is intended for Key Stage 2 classroom teachers who will have pupils with a range of differing needs within their class. Observation and assessment must be practicable, relevant and of specific use with regard to planning work, making informed decisions about classroom groupings and monitoring progress. It should also be consistent with school policies. For example, a school's assessment policy might detail school-based assessment arrangements for tracking progress in core subjects, and there might be screening arrangements in place to provide benchmark information about pupils on entry to Key Stage 2 or at transition. Such arrangements might be detailed within the English Policy and there are likely to be links with the school's SEN policy. The school's SEN co-ordinator will be involved with any pupils at Stages 2 and above of *The Code* and may be carrying out regular tests. Any further assessment by the class teacher should be complementary and not compromise other assessments which may be planned or ongoing. There is a real danger of pupils becoming 'over-assessed' and the 'practice effect' of administering any standardised tests too frequently might make the results unreliable.

How should a pupil's reading difficulties be assessed?
A comprehensive and detailed profile of the learner is needed before starting to plan a teaching programme which provides the necessary learning opportunities which will enable pupils to acquire effective reading strategies. Such a profile will include their approach to print, their strengths and weaknesses and some indication of how they are performing compared with other pupils of their age. If we adapt the model suggested by *The Code* with this purpose in mind, it might read as follows:

- gather relevant background information about the pupil's reading difficulties
- plan appropriate activities to promote the acquisition of a range of reading strategies
- monitor and review and record the pupil's progress.

The gathering of relevant background and assessment information and the monitoring/reviewing of progress now needs to be discussed in more detail. The planning of appropriate activities will be discussed in later chapters.

Gathering relevant assessment information
This can be broken down into several component parts:

1. background assessment
2. observational assessment
3. the evaluation of reading performance (standardised tests, criterion referenced tests, non-standardised assessment)
4. further diagnostic work (sub-skills).

1. Background assessment
This will include some information gathering and much of this will already be readily available in school. Parents and the pupils themselves can also provide valuable information which can help to establish a wide-ranging picture of the learner and there may be details of medical and other information such as speech therapy reports which will contribute to a teacher's understanding of the pupil's needs.

Such an assessment might also include:

- Key Stage 1 assessment information
- results of any standardised/criterion referenced tests
- information from previous teacher(s).

2. Observational assessment
Curriculum time is at a premium and it is imperative therefore that time is used efficiently to maximum effect. There may still be teachers who worry about how they will fit in 'hearing readers'. However, time must be balanced and the teacher needs to ensure that there is adequate coverage of the National Curriculum although this is being slimmed down and there is more time now available for basic skills. The ability to read is a vital skill and it is therefore essential that there is a clear understanding on the part of teachers of the complexity of the reading process and of the individual but integrated processes involved. Henrietta Dombey (1992) points out that:

> [pupils] need to experience reading time as focused and productive, as time when they learn a number of different lessons that combine to help them make meaning from written texts.

Teachers are becoming increasingly aware that 'hearing readers', though important, is not the be-all and end-all of teaching reading. As Keith Lloyd, head of OFSTED's Primary Team, has said, 'Hearing them read is not the same thing as teaching them to read.' Individual time spent with a pupil should be productive and it should be carefully planned for.

Consider using just such an individual session with a pupil to carry out a detailed reading observation. By using a checklist (Figure 1) which can be ticked or underlined whilst the pupil is reading to the teacher, a wealth of information about approaches and responses to text can be determined. This will provide the class teacher with detailed knowledge of how the pupil is operating with text. It provides the kind of qualitative information which will help teachers to make more sensitive judgements when planning programmes of work. Whilst observational assessments provide a 'snapshot in time' and tell us how a pupil is performing on a given day, in a given set of circumstances, the record kept can be referred to again at a later date and compared with subsequent assessments to check whether progress is being made.

READING OBSERVATION SHEET

Name: ....   **D.O.B.** ....

Class: ....   **Date:** ....

- **Information Gathering** (✓ to indicate if other relevant information pertains)

medical information e.g.

hearing ☐ *wears spectacles* ☐ *other visual problems* ☐ *other* ☐

information from: *previous teacher(s)* ☐ *pupil* ☐ *parents/carers* ☐

information from other professionals: *(e.g. speech therapist)* ☐ ....

- **Concepts about Print:**

terminology - ✓ if pupil can identify/name:
book title, front, back, first page, word, letter, full stop, paragraph, last, top, bottom

meaning of punctuation
can recognise and respond to [. , ? ! ''] *within the text.*
Can explain function of [. , ? ! '']

tracking *(correct orientation from top to bottom* ☐ *and left to right* ☐ *)*

- **General Response to Text:** (underline all that apply)
attitude:
confident   keen to try   anxious   lacks confidence   lacks motivation

perseverance:
good   average   poor (gives up easily)

level of dependence:
independent   requires some support   dependent on support

awareness of own performance:
aware   some awareness   little/no awareness

level of concentration:
good   average   poor (easily distracted)

(Continued)

Figure 1
© J. Calver, S. Ranson, D. Smith (1999)   This page may be photocopied

11

- **Oral Reading:** (underline all that apply)

rate: *fluent pace*   *fluency developing*   *slow/hesitant*

expression: *good use of expression*   *emerging/some use*   *yet to develop*

confidence: *willing to tackle text*   *will sometimes attempt*   *reluctant to try*

awareness of sentence boundaries: ☐

- **Response to Unfamiliar Words:** (underline all that apply)
makes wild guesses
reads on
willing to attempt words
studies text carefully/makes impulsive responses
makes sound/symbol confusions
uses contextual/picture cues
attempts decoding (phonic analysis): occasionally/frequently
makes semantic substitutions (e.g. 'grass' for 'garden')
makes visual substitutions based on structural similarity (whether/where)
makes syntactic substitutions (e.g. 'The dog ran for the 'ball' - not the 'stick')

- **Ability to Gain Meaning from Text:** (underline all that apply)
able to talk about story line
can explain/describe/predict
answers questions about text:
  from general knowledge/without recourse to text/verbatim from text
uses stock responses to open-ended questions
misinterprets questions
lacks confidence in answering

- **Additional comments:**

Records can be updated using the same checklist and recording in a new colour as frequently as required (possibly half-termly).

Such a record would enable staff to identify any gaps in basic concepts (e.g. whether the pupil is clear about what constitutes a 'word' and a 'letter'). This will assist the teacher in setting relevant and appropriate targets which can also form the basis for the individual discussion/conference with each pupil envisaged in *The National Literacy Strategy*, lasting approximately 10 minutes and carried out each half-term (as a minimum). Pupils are likely to do better if they understand which areas need targeting and what action they can take to help themselves. This collaborative approach avoids learning taking place within a vacuum where teaching is regarded as something which is 'done to' the pupil who often has only the remotest idea about its purpose.

The gathering of relevant background information and a Reading Observation may well provide the teacher with enough knowledge about the pupil to set relevant targets and plan suitable learning opportunities. However, it may also be necessary to investigate a pupil's reading difficulties further if a teacher suspects there may be more deep-seated difficulties.

3. Evaluation of reading performance
The use of standardised tests

Standardised tests have been used for many years. They are designed to test a pupil's performance against other pupils of a similar age. Test items are constructed and then given a trial run using large samples of pupils from a range of educational backgrounds (urban/rural/state/independent etc.). The results are then used to produce norms which can be used to interpret individual results. Most standardised tests have a standard deviation of 15. The average score would be 100, and 15 points either way (85–115) would indicate the average range expected on a normal distribution curve. Thus one can check whether a pupil's reading is within the average range or below that level. These tests can of course similarly identify more able pupils, though it should be remembered that reading ability is not the best indicator of overall general ability. Sometimes schools use a cut-off point below which pupils would be screened more thoroughly e.g. below a standardised score of 85 or 80 depending on the profile of the year group/school population. Standardised scores should not be confused with percentile rankings where ratings of 1–100 are used. A percentile rating of 30 would indicate that a pupil is functioning at a level as well as or better than 30 other pupils out of any 100 pupils in the general population and that 70 pupils out of 100 would be expected to do better.

There are group tests of reading ability which can be given to whole classes or groups of pupils. These can screen an intake or a particular cohort. Such tests may indicate certain pupils who will need to be looked at more closely. This is when an individual test can be used to identify particular strengths and weaknesses.

A note of caution

Whilst standardised tests have their uses, they also have drawbacks and these must be considered when using them.

Uses:

- standardised tests provide an objective assessment related to national norms. They give an indication of how pupils are performing against other pupils of their age
- tests provide standardised and age equivalent scores
- they can be used over a period of time to measure progress
- they can provide a profile of the class/school population
- they can be used to identify those falling below a specified 'intervention' level
- they can be used to evaluate the success of intervention programmes
- they can be used for passing pupil information to subsequent schools.

Drawbacks:
- tests vary and so do results – different tests have different basals (base-lines and ceilings) and cannot be directly compared
- the standardisation sample may not be of a comparable group (the technical data provided for tests should not be ignored when deciding on which tests to use in school)
- the standardisation may be quite old and the sample tested would therefore reflect the educational focus of the time
- reading ages tell us nothing about the strategies being used – nor do they indicate courses of action
- results can be imbued with a great deal of status (sometimes inappropriately so) – they provide a snapshot of how a pupil performed on that test on a particular occasion
- there are ethical issues to be considered – are parents aware that tests are being used? Who sees the results? What are the results used for? If results are used as an indicator for allocating resources has (or should) this have been discussed with parents?
- be aware of the limitations of the test that is used and have a clear idea of the purpose of testing.

Final note

In order to provide additional information from the Key Stage 2 Standard Assessment Test (SAT) results, standardised scores are now available for reading (along with spelling and maths). These are for optional use.

Criterion referenced assessment

This enables teachers to judge a pupil's performance against a specified set of criteria. The most commonly used will be the level descriptors for the National Curriculum attainment targets in each subject and teachers will be familiar with matching performance to these criteria. Other examples may be found within published materials, where checklists and criteria are set out. These are often arranged in a developmental sequence and can assist staff in setting targets. Key word lists and phonic checksheets will also be familiar to most Key Stage 2 teachers and are an integral part of *The National Literacy Strategy*. These assessments are non-standardised though they enable teachers to keep a cumulative record of achievement against certain criteria and can also be useful in assessing rates of progress.

4. Further diagnostic assessment

There may be occasions when a pupil is experiencing reading difficulties and the teacher will need information of a more detailed kind to determine what skills and strategies the pupil is bringing to the reading process. More in-depth, diagnostic assessment of this type will help to pinpoint strengths and weaknesses in the sub-skills which are essential for fluent, automatic reading. One needs to think back to the discussions raised in the first section of this book. Reading is a complex cognitive process. A mature reader uses different cueing systems when attempting to gain meaning from print:

- *grapho-phonic* – matching the look of a letter (or letters) with its sound. Those with no knowledge of Italian will find the sentence '*mi piace il chianti*' hard to read unless they have been taught that in this sequence of letters '*c*' is pronounced as '*ch*' and '*ch*' is pronounced as '*k*' (that is, unless they just enjoy red wine).
- *syntactic* – using knowledge of grammatical structure/word order
'Ann said that ------- did not like sprouts' (the missing word could be a name e.g. 'Robert' or a pronoun e.g. 'she').
'Ann said that s---- did not like sprouts' (the first letter as it is lower case helps us to predict the missing word with greater accuracy – 'she').

- *semantic* – using the content of the passage to make sense
  'but she does like fish and ------- with plenty of salt and -------'.

Reading skill involves decoding words on the page and making informed predictions. The experienced reader will probably confirm expectations by using context and syntactical constraints, rather than by the literal decoding of every word. It is useful to know how nearly the young reader approximates to the tactics of an experienced reader.

How to recognise and record which strategies are being used
The Reading Observation Checklist will already have alerted teachers to the pupil's general approach to reading – their response to unfamiliar words, the contextual or other strategies that they favour. *Miscue analysis* is a widely accepted way of looking at the reading process and one which reflects its complexity.

The uses of miscue analysis
- it provides for a qualitative analysis of reading behaviour and looks in more detail at the strategies that the pupil brings to the reading process
- it allows the teacher to make judgements at a finer linguistic level
- results are not standardised – there are no norms. The reader's development is diagnosed by qualitative analysis of the reading of different passages at suitable intervals
- whilst judgements will be subjective, it is the general pattern of the pupil's functioning as a reader that is of interest
- errors (miscues) are not necessarily regarded as 'bad' or in need of remediation. They are necessary for qualitative analysis. They indicate symptoms of possible mental processes which can be positive or negative.

What purpose would miscue analysis have for the Key Stage 2 classroom teacher?
- to observe whether the readers are using all the cueing systems available and to see to what extent they are approaching the text as mature, fluent readers
- to pinpoint developmental stages in reading acquisition and to intervene appropriately where necessary
- to gain a measure of the extent to which the reader is reading 'for meaning' (using context cues), in addition to or as an alternative to giving comprehension questions
- as a window on listening to pupils read which helps the teacher approach it with informed attitudes, making the exercise more fruitful.

How to carry out a miscue analysis
Whilst some standardised reading tests utilise this approach (for example *The Neale Analysis, The Individual Reading Analysis* and *The New Reading Analysis*, NFER-Nelson) any passage may be used provided it allows the reader to make enough errors for the purpose of analysis. A scheme reader chosen to allow the pupil considerable success and consolidation is unlikely to be suitable for the purpose of a miscue analysis. Pupils meet texts at three levels of difficulty; at an *independent* level the pupil would be expected to cope well with 90–95 per cent of the text. At an *instructional* level the pupil would meet enough new words to require them to practise their word attack strategies, but they would still be able to read enough of the text to derive a reasonable level of meaning from it and be able to cope with 80–90 per cent of the text. At *frustrational* level the pupil encounters so many new or unknown words that any sense of reading for meaning is compromised (coping with less than 80 per cent of the text). The passage chosen for analysis must be at an instructional level so that the pupil's strategies in dealing with unknown words can be observed (this might be 20 errors in every 100 words read). A form of miscue analysis is used in the end of Key Stage 2 assessment tasks for pupils being assessed at

Level 2. A running record grid allows the teacher to record omissions, self-corrections and miscues which demonstrate the strategies being used (phonic, graphic, syntactic and contextual). Teachers may therefore decide to use these blank grids and a similar notation to record any informal assessments they carry out.

Alternatively, once a passage has been selected, photocopy (and enlarge) the section of text to provide a record sheet on which the teacher can record the pupil's reading errors. As the pupil reads, the errors are recorded using a form of short-hand devised by the teacher. Practice will help teachers to develop the symbols they feel most comfortable with; alternatively, the following model (based on the NFER-Nelson tests) may be used.

substitution	It was *party* pretty late at night
insertion	It was ∧*not* pretty late at night
omission	It was [pretty] late at night
reversal (word)	It saw pretty late at night
reversal (word order)	It│was pretty late at night
refusal	It was pretty late at night
hesitation	It was pretty/late at night
repetition	It was pretty late at night
decoding	It was ✓✓✓ pretty late at night
self-correction	It was *plenty* pretty late at night

Once the passage has been read and the errors recorded by the teacher, it will be possible to analyse the balance of miscues. All oral readers make mistakes from time to time – even fluent and accomplished silent readers may omit words, reverse the order or substitute words when reading aloud for an audience. If mistakes do not change the meaning of the passage the errors may be deemed 'positive' – possibly indicating that the text is being mentally assimilated and reproduced orally in a slightly different form. Accuracy is not therefore the absolute criterion of success in reading aloud. Indeed, some pupils may appear to read quite inaccurately, yet still manage to gain a high level of meaning from the text.

Some errors, however, will be regarded as 'negative' in that they inhibit understanding, e.g. a pupil who uses a visual approach to reading and makes spontaneous guesses based on some structural similarity as in reading 'house' for 'horse' will have difficulty in making sense of the text.

Such an analysis will provide the teacher with valuable insight into how the pupil is approaching the reading process. If a purely visual approach is being used, such a pupil might well have appeared to cope at Key Stage 1, relying on a basic sight vocabulary and a familiarity with controlled scheme readers which allows for a high level of prediction based on repetition.

Alternatively, pupils who rely solely on structural decoding to the point where they attempt to decode even irregular key words may have a weak visual memory and may need a programme of support activities designed to develop this skill area. Pupils will have their own pattern of strengths and weaknesses. Having carried out such an analysis the teacher will have a much greater awareness of which skills pupils will need to develop and which approaches are likely to be more successful.

Consider the following miscue analysis which was carried out on Jane, a Year 4 pupil of 8 years 10 months with a reading age assessed at 7 years 4 months, some 18 months behind her chronological age.

Miscue Analysis
(Passage taken from *Fantastic Mr. Fox* by Roald Dahl.)

His black nose twitched from side to side, sniffing and sniffing for the scent [sneck] of danger.

He found none [no], and he was just about to go trotting [toffing] forward into the wood when [t] he heard

or thought he heard a tiny [thing] noise, a soft rustling [softly / stirring] sound, as though [following] someone had moved a

foot [fote] ever [never] so gently [glently] through [fort] a patch of dry leaves.

Mr. Fox flattened [flated] his body against [ag] the ground and lay very still, his ears pricked [picked].

He waited a long time, but he heard nothing more.

'It must have been a field-mouse', he told himself, 'or some other small animal.'

Analysis
- Jane's errors totalled 17 per cent of the passage.
- She used decoding strategies on 10 per cent of the words – sometimes she was able to synthesise the whole word, but not always. Sometimes she was not able to hold all sounds in her head with the end result that words were missing essential sounds ('picked' instead of 'pricked', 'flated' instead of 'flattened').
- Sometimes Jane transposed letters, indicating some visual sequencing difficulties ('glently' for 'gently', 'sneck' for 'scent').
- Her reading of 'trotting' as 'toffing' is possibly as a result of directional confusion of the 't/f'.
- In addition, there were some visual errors based on structural similarity to the stimulus word ('thing' for 'tiny', 'never' for 'ever' and 'then' for 'when').

Ways in which to plan a programme of support using assessment information will be discussed in later chapters. Teachers will need to consider how they will present this assessment to their pupils. It will be important to discuss its purpose and also the results. This can be a positive experience in that it fosters an awareness in the pupil that there are strategies which can be learned and acquired. It helps them to take some responsibility for their own learning. Target setting can then be negotiated between the teacher and pupil and there can be more active involvement if the pupil can be encouraged to monitor and record any success (this might be sight vocabulary words, or certain letter strings or phonic units mastered).

PART 2 - Reading approaches
1 - Teaching reading through visual strategies

One of the key skills in the National Curriculum Programme of Study for reading at Key Stage 2 states:

> To increase their ability to read with fluency, accuracy, understanding and enjoyment, pupils should be taught to extend their phonic and graphic knowledge to include more complex patterns and irregularities.

In order to address the teaching of visual strategies the following aims will be considered in this section:

- to examine strategies to develop automatic sight recognition in order to improve fluency
- to consider methods for increasing sight vocabulary at Key Stage 2.

Our objective when teaching pupils to read is for them to become fluent readers using minimal clues. Examine the following sentences that were written by a Year 5 pupil as part of a storybook for a younger pupil:

~~They went into every toy store they passed. The teddies were either too big or too small for Sophie.~~

~~Then they passed one shop called Lovely Teddies. They had a look around and Sophie's eye caught sight of one special teddy bear which they bought.~~

Chrismas eev wos a long nite for Sofey becos she wos looking forwod to oll her prezance.

These sentences show how we are able to read text even when parts of the words are missing, or the words spelt incorrectly. (It is, however, easier to read words when the upper coastlines give the visual clues.) In order to achieve this, fluent readers use the following skills:

- rapid scanning sequencing – looking at the shape of the word rather than every letter, e.g. nose/noise
- visual recognition – automatic sight recognition of the words on the page
- context.

Factors relating to reading fluency

Let us examine some of the areas which need to be considered if a pupil is having difficulty developing visual strategies:

- *Good vision* – the class teacher needs to be alerted to the fact that pupils in the class may not be seeing the print too clearly. Sight checks are no longer carried out routinely in school but if you feel there is a potential problem either ask the school nurse to check (with parent's/carer's permission) or ask the parent/carer to take the pupil to an optometrist. Sight checks for pupils continue to be free of charge (at the time of going to print) and this may be worth mentioning to parents. Some pupils have difficulty tracking the text along a straight line, have problems with the contrast of black print on white pages and find reading a very tiring exercise. These pupils may have a particular problem with their vision and should be referred to a screener for Scotopic Sensitivity Syndrome, sometimes called Irlen Syndrome. For further information read *Reading by the Colors* by Helen Irlen (1991).

- *Good sight recognition* – this must be an automatic response. Pupils who sound out each letter individually may be able to provide the correct word but their sight recognition should be considered weak.
- *Visual discrimination* – this is matching shapes, letters and words with increasing levels of difficulty. Identifying letter patterns within words and making associations with words is a necessary skill.
- *Visual memory* – pupils need to have the ability to recall the word again in another part of the text.
- *Rapid scanning sequencing* – this is the skill that fluent readers use when they focus on part of the word rather than the whole word in order to read it.
- *Graphemic awareness* – the ability to see words within words and use this as a strategy to enable the word to be read. Making word associations is also included so that if the pupils can read 'could' they should be able to read 'would' and 'should'.
- *Language* – understanding the structure of spoken language and the ability to use the correct tense alongside a wide vocabulary will enhance a pupil's ability to recognise whether a word is correct within the context.

How can this be achieved?

In the initial stages of learning to read, pupils will be introduced to words which are particularly relevant to them, probably their home, family and school. Whilst this remains an option for some pupils at Key Stage 2 (through a topic the pupil may be particularly interested in, e.g. football) it is likely that for most older pupils the vocabulary they are introduced to will come from a reading scheme or sets of carefully graded books which may be colour coded. Alongside this core vocabulary they will need to increase their knowledge of high frequency words from a chosen list. Many lists are available but schools may decide to use those included in *The National Literacy Strategy* as a starting point. Pupils will need to have some understanding of graphemes (the written representation of a sound) and be able to develop the use of contextual cues.

How reading schemes can reinforce visual strategies

Reading schemes can provide the teacher working with pupils at Key Stage 2, who are experiencing difficulties in developing visual strategies for reading:

- a clear structure for the teaching of reading. New vocabulary is introduced in a controlled way and builds on what has already been introduced
- books graded into a series of coded or numbered levels which may facilitate the ability to group pupils together for certain activities
- a related programme of language work which helps to structure other reading activities. Support work enables pupils with learning difficulties to consolidate vocabulary which has already been introduced through other methods, e.g. word games
- an opportunity to monitor rates of progress
- familiar texts, characters and situations.

Other written material, stories, information books, rhymes, poems, songs, riddles, comics and books created by the pupils themselves provide the broader reading experience.

Choosing reading materials

Whether pupils read from a reading scheme book when they are reading to the class teacher or choose from a range of graded books, they should be encouraged to explore a range of reading material. By the time pupils reach Key Stage 2 they want to look as though they are reading the same material as their peers. Indeed, some parents feel they should be reading books which have chapters. In order to choose reading books at an appropriate interest level but which match the pupil's readability level teachers may need to consider checking NASEN's *A-Z* for appropriate books of higher interest levels but with lower reading levels. The books listed are graded according to phase, interest age and reading level. The purpose of the book is to facilitate the choice and organisation of reading resources so that they can be effectively matched to the individual needs of young readers. There is a complementary CD-ROM designed to assist teachers with their choice of books.

Teachers attending an INSET session compiled the following list, which is not exhaustive:

Books	*Reading level*	*Interest level*	*Publisher*
High Stakes Adventures	7–8 and 8–9	10–16	LDA
Ten Minutes Thrillers	8	9+	LDA
Five Minute Thrillers	9	10–16	LDA
Skyways	6–9	8–12+	Collins
Rescue Readers	7–10	8–14	Ginn
Jets	6.6–7.5	6–11	Collins
Impact	6–9	10–14	Ginn
Wellington Square	6–8.5	7–13+	Nelson
Penguin Plays	6.6–8.0	7–11	Ginn
Zapper	6–8	10+	Ginn

Strategies for improving visual skills for reading
At Key Stage 1 pupils are likely to have experienced a range of activities aimed at developing their visual skills. These activities used at Key Stage 1 may need to be continued and extended at Key Stage 2, especially for those pupils in Year 3.

Visual discrimination at Key Stage 1
- matching games
- classifying objects by shape, colour or size
- completing pictures of shapes and objects
- looking at 'busy' pictures, picking out objects
- recognising a picture as it is gradually revealed
- dominoes – symbols and pictures
- lotto – symbols and pictures
- snap
- mosaics, jigsaws, pegboard activities, multi-link pictures.

Visual discrimination at Key Stage 2
- identifying the 'odd one out', e.g. O O O A O; C C G C C; dpb bpd dpb dpb
- how many times can you find a particular letter (be specific and write it on the paper) in one minute? Highlighter pens can be used for this activity with each letter identified in a different colour
- pairing letter cards, moving on to words. Increase the level of difficulty gradually
- letter/word dominoes.

Matching at Key Stage 1
  • matching letters/words – snap, Bingo, dominoes, pelmanism (pairs), programs for use with the Concept Keyboard.

Matching at Key Stage 2
  • as above
  • word walls (e.g. taken from *Wellington Square* published by Nelson) can be used for matching single words
  • sentences which are photocopied so the pupil can match the words to the sentence. At first use the same font. Later extension activities can use different fonts, including handwritten material.

Tracing over print at Key Stages 1 and 2
  • see multi-sensory teaching on page 34.

Rebus symbols at Key Stages 1 and 2
Rebus symbols are pictorial representations of whole words. There are various glossaries containing symbols that are commonly used (e.g. Mayer-Johnson Picture Communication Symbols, Writing with Symbols 2000). The LDA Rebus Glossary contains a list of about a thousand words (Van Oosteroom and Devereux, 1992). It may prove particularly helpful to support pupils who are finding it difficult to learn a sight vocabulary by making flash cards that incorporate the symbol as well as the word. It is useful in the learning of high frequency words which are otherwise difficult to illustrate.

Research has shown that where pictures are used alongside words the learner makes pleasing progress. (See Moran, Smith, Meads and Beck, 1996.)

Both nouns and key words are shown in the glossary; here are some examples:

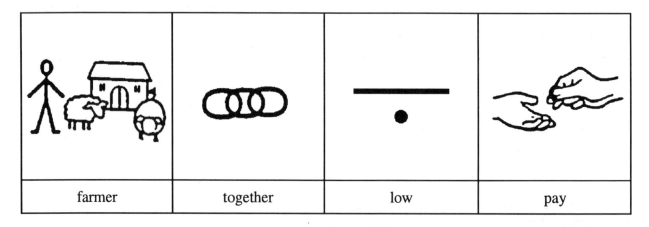

| farmer | together | low | pay |

It is important to note that although various glossaries exist schools have also developed their own sets of symbols to match their particular needs. It would be useful to consider using symbols for History, Geography and Science topics as well as the high frequency words from *The National Literacy Strategy*.

The Writing Set (Widget) has been developed as a word processing package using the rebus symbols. Speech is built into the program allowing words to be read as they are entered, or to be read afterwards.

Precision testing at Key Stage 1 and 2
This can be used to help acquire a larger sight vocabulary. Decide upon the vocabulary: core words from reading books, key words, topic-related words etc. and create a blank grid like the one included in the appendix.

The procedure is:

a. choose three unknown words the pupil would like to read regardless of length or degree of difficulty. There may need to be some degree of censorship
b. choose another two words already known as sight words
c. set out the grid (or probe sheet) by filling in the five words across the first line, then again in random order for the next four lines
d. teach the unknown words in any of the ways already suggested, e.g. word games of snap, bingo, dominoes, pairs etc. The words can be practised at home
e. at each 'testing' session check the words for exactly one minute – tick each correct word and fill in the total number known each day
f. check for one week
g. change words each week but keep two of the learned words as the 'known' words and add three new ones.

Further probe sheets will be needed and a stop watch or timer. In the appendix there is a probe sheet which has been filled in. These are topic-related words which the pupil needs to learn to read in order to use them in the work.

Using the *Breakthrough to Literacy* (D. Moyle) approach

The use of a *Breakthrough* folder (which contains small flashcards of commonly used words) may not appeal to pupils in Key Stage 2 in the original Sentence Maker format but a smaller folder with words which the pupil is working on might be worth considering. Ideally you need a mini-sized *Breakthrough* folder which could contain topic-related words alongside key words being taught. The words can be used in order to develop independent writing skills.

Other suggestions

As previously mentioned, research has shown how linking words to pictures (visual cues) can help pupils who have failed to acquire a sight vocabulary. For more information see Moran et al, 1996. The following is a summary of their research which could be adapted for use in schools with pupils at Key Stage 2 who are experiencing difficulties in acquiring visual strategies.

- For the purposes of the research two teachers who worked in two primary schools with 12 pupils were chosen.
- A basic checklist of 100 words was administered before and after intervention. (These teachers used SNAP Basic Skills Checklist 1996 but others might be equally suitable.)
- The pupils were given a short individual teaching session of ten minutes, three times a week for seven weeks.
- The teacher chose five words to be learned at a time and wrote them on pieces of card.
- Using another card, the pupil was asked to make up a sentence to include the word and to draw a picture to illustrate the sentence. The teacher wrote the sentence again on the back of this card.
- Each school used a different method. In School 1, the sentences were made up and the pictures drawn by the pupils. In School 2 the pupils struggled to make up sentences themselves so the teacher did it for them. The procedures were the same – time was spent practising the word and sentence and then using the picture to learn them.
- The results showed increases in the number of words known. Where the more personal method was used the average number of words learned in seven weeks was 40. The average number of words learned in seven weeks using the more teacher-directed method was 15.

The quality of drawings did not appear to have any significant negative effect upon learning. Teachers found the ten-minute session too short for them to teach five words.

Learning key words through 'onset and rime'
Consider the three-letter words, which are taught using one of the lists of high frequency words. Identify the 'key word' and add other words which are in the same rime family.

> e.g. but – hut, cut, nut, rut
> > now – cow, how, bow, row
> > big – pig, fig, wig, rig, jig
> > can – man, pan, ran, ban, tan
> > did – hid, bid, lid, kid
> > get – let, wet, net, set, met
> > new – few, pew

Move on to four and five-letter words. Whilst a number of key words may not increase at a rapid rate, it is to be hoped that the pupil will identify a pattern when confronted with unknown words. There is a link between visual memory acquisition and using analogies from one sound pattern to another. Pupils may find visual letter strings which do not conform to the rime. These irregularities need to be pointed out and discussed so that the pupils become more aware of the complexities of the English language (e.g. in the above 'how' list both 'bow' and 'row' have two pronunciations).

Use of Information Communication Technology
New software is being developed all the time and teachers will need to consult the most up-to-date catalogues for further information and request demonstration disks which are usually available. The annual ICT (BETT exhibition) held in London provides an excellent opportunity to view and try out new programs.

Concept keyboard – Word program – SEMERC
Overlays are produced using words and pictures. By touching the words or pictures pupils are able to write sentences using the vocabulary which is being introduced.

Clicker – Crick Publishing Ltd.
This is an on-screen keyboard with speech. Each cell can hold a letter, word, phrase or picture. When the pupil clicks on a cell in Clicker using either the mouse or touch screen the text is sent to the program. Text, pictures and speech can be used to create grids. Creating new grids gives access to a larger vocabulary.

Pupils who start to read by learning a sight vocabulary in Key Stage 1 without developing their auditory skills are often those pupils who begin to have difficulty at Key Stage 2 because they have insufficient strategies for attempting unknown words. The next part of this section examines ways of extending phonic knowledge at Key Stage 2.

2 - Teaching reading through auditory strategies

Why teach phonics?

Evidence shows that pupils begin learning to read by using a combination of strategies. They guess and predict words from context and from their developing awareness of grammatical structures, whilst using a mainly word-recognition approach to individual words. The careful, graded introduction of vocabulary through early scheme books helps facilitate these skills. However, unless this early approach has been complemented by structured and systematic teaching of phonics, which teaches the pupil about the alphabetic sound/symbol system of English, young readers often encounter problems later on. By Key Stage 2 an over-reliance on exclusively visual and contextual strategies can no longer support the reading tasks which pupils will experience. Throughout Key Stage 2 the predictability of the texts they will meet will diminish and the range of vocabulary will increase. Not only will vocabulary be extended to cover a range of uses and audiences but subject specific vocabulary will increase as pupils are introduced to new concepts and experiences.

What a pupil will be expected to know on entry to Key Stage 2

The National Literacy Strategy details the specific phonic (and spelling) work to be covered in Years 1 to 6. Pupils will be expected to have covered a considerable amount of ground in Key Stage 1 so that they are competent in using phonic strategies by the time they reach Key Stage 2. It is anticipated that they will have a practical understanding and awareness of:

- initial sounds and the ability to write and read these in different positions within words
- short vowel sounds (CVC words, consonant-vowel-consonant)
- initial consonant clusters (blends) and end clusters (e.g. ck, ft, lk, mp etc.)
- long vowel phonemes (digraphs) – ee, ea, ai, oa etc.
- common spelling patterns for vowel phonemes (digraphs e.g. ar, oy, ow) and later trigraphs (e.g. air, ear).

Using assessment information to determine where reading difficulties lie

There are many pupils at Key Stage 2 who are not yet proficient at this level and may only have an imperfect understanding of how the phono-graphic (sound/symbol) system of English is constructed. The earlier chapter on assessment discussed ways for the classroom teacher to identify a pupil's reading difficulties in more detail. If the Reading Observation Sheet (see Figure 1 on pages 11-12) and/or the more diagnostic miscue analysis (referred to on pages 15-17) reveals that a pupil is failing to use phonic strategies, teachers will need to ask themselves some further questions. They will need to know if the pupils have the prerequisite skills to enable them to use this approach. In other words, do they have a level of phonological awareness which will enable them to interpret and make sense of the sound system of the English language?

Phonological awareness

Phonological awareness refers to the ability to focus specifically on features of speech sounds. *The National Literacy Strategy* defines it as an awareness of sounds within words and which can be demonstrated by an ability to generate rhyme (*way, say, may*), alliteration (*great, green, grasshoppers*) and helps in segmenting and blending the component sounds (*st-ick, de-part-ment*). This forms a basis for a further level of awareness which links the speech sounds with the graphemes (letters or letter patterns). Once pupils understand that writing is the abstract representation of the spoken language and that the individual speech sounds can be recorded by letters and groups of letters, then they are ready to start developing phonetic strategies to assist their reading of text. In their comprehensive book on phonological awareness Layton, Deeny and Upton (1997) state:

An awareness that spoken language can be broken into segments is obligatory if individuals are going to read and spell effectively. Research evidence only supports and explains what numerous teachers of pupils with literacy difficulties have noticed for years.

Many researchers (Goswami and Bryant (1990) and Goswami (1995)) have investigated the role of phonological awareness in a pupil's developing literacy skills and have focused on how pupils can be helped to make the connection between speech sounds and spelling patterns.

One important research finding in recent years has centred on the different levels of phonological awareness. The traditional view held that spoken words could be broken down into syllables or phonemes:

SYLLABLES	PHONEMES
cob/web	/c/ + /o/ + /b/ - /w/ + /e/ + /b/
pig/let	/p/ + /i/ + /g/ - /l/ + /e/ + /t/

In this instance, the individual phonemes correspond to discrete letters of the alphabet. However, this task becomes more complex when dealing with words where the phonemes do not correspond to single letters as in s/oa/p, c/a/tch, sh/i/p and l/igh/t which also have three phonemes. Phonemes (units of single sound) may be formed by different combinations of graphemes:

- a graph - a single letter e.g. 'f' as in *fat*
- a digraph - two letters e.g. *green* or *much*
- a trigraph - three letters e.g. *bridge* or *witch*.

In some cases longer sequences of four letters (quadrographs) can produce a single phoneme e.g. *eighty* or *although*.

Children who do not understand that this happens will find reading very confusing if they pursue a 'one letter makes one sound' approach (s/o/a/p/ and s/h/i/p/) and try to sound out the individual letters.

More recently, linguists have determined an intermediate level of phonological awareness between the syllable and the phoneme that divides words into two units constituting the 'onset' - the initial consonant(s) and the 'rime' - the vowel sound and final consonants which follow it. Thus 'rime' endings have the same spelling pattern (pig/wig/big/dig), unlike rhymes which do not necessarily do so (care/where/fair).

WORD	ONSET + RIME		
pig	p	+	ig
trip	tr	+	ip

Research has shown that onset and rime is psychologically distinguishable long before the pupil learns to read. Awareness of rime alerts pupils to the possibility of making analogies between spelling patterns in words when they begin learning to read. If one can read the word '*day*' and recognise the pattern of letters, then one might be able to predict '*ray*' and '*hay*' by making an analogy with the word (*day*) which is already known. Consider the word '*fight*' – this is an irregular word in terms of the individual phonemes that make up the spelling pattern (f/i/g/h/t) but as a word, it is highly consistent in terms of the rime ending – there are 90 words in English that use the letter string '*ight*' with no exceptions in pronunciation. Therefore, a pupil who begins to learn to read by segmenting words into onsets and rimes is at an advantage.

```
early experiences with rhyme
        ↓
awareness of onset and rime units
        ↓
use of analogies in reading
```

The pupil with poor phonological awareness

Some of the factors which might contribute to poor acquisition of phonological skills have already been discussed. Early hearing impairment or intermittent glue ear can also be a common problem. Pupils may have missed out on crucial experience and training early on as a result of this condition. If it is discovered through assessment that a pupil has poor phonological awareness or finds it difficult to discriminate between sounds (not just those which are commonly confused such as f/th as in *thunder/funder* and v/th as in *clothes/cloves*) then it is always worth having hearing checked to see if it is within normal limits.

It may also be that a pupil is aware of rhyme (*bat/fat/cat*), alliteration (*fast, furious, ferocious, football*), syllables (*pic/nic*) etc. but through over-reliance on other (often visual) strategies, has not developed the skills which would help them to utilise this knowledge of sounds. Other pupils again may not have been able to pick up on much of this earlier work and may require more structured and explicit teaching. Pupils who find learning difficult are unlikely to be able to deduce things for themselves: providing experiences will not be sufficient for them to develop the necessary skills without structured and focused teaching.

This is when the use of non-standardised assessment techniques will help the teacher to pinpoint where a pupil's difficulties lie. Knowledge regarding the pupil's awareness of rhyme, alliteration, syllable and onset and rime divisions will be very important in planning activities which may be needed to promote acquisition of these skills. It is perhaps easier to see how the oral activities which promote phonological awareness can be incorporated into the preschool or early years setting where songs, rhymes and oral games form an essential part of the curriculum. At Key Stage 2 the challenge is to provide supporting activities which will help the pupils to develop their phonological skills whilst being fun and maintaining their often fragile self-esteem intact. Activities must be appropriate to the pupil's age and stage of social development. A range of ideas covering both oral and table-top games and activities follows.

Some Ideas for Developing Phonological Awareness at Key Stage 2

CIRCLE GAMES
Word Chains
Names/words beginning with ... (reinforces alliteration)
- pupils sit in a circle (or their usual seating arrangement)
- a category is selected (e.g. football teams, girls' names, food etc.)
- each pupil gives a name in turn until they are forced to drop out (no repetitions)
  e.g. *sausages, spaghetti, sweets, salami, sprouts.*

I know a word that sounds like ... (reinforces rhyme)
- choose any word (perhaps featuring a particular rime ending you have been concentrating on)
- pupils each provide a rhyming word until they drop out leaving a winner (e.g. *trip, flip, drip, slip, chip, whip*).
  For variation, set a time limit and appoint a time-keeper with a small gong or similar.

Letter links (reinforces alliteration)
- choose a word to start with
- then each pupil in turn thinks of a word which must begin with the final letter of the preceding word (no repeats) until a winner remains e.g. *grass, sun, nest, trap, pig, garden.*
(If the end letter is unvoiced such as *note* the next pupil will have to give a word starting with the last sounded letter e.g. *note, ten.*)

Alphabet categories (reinforces initial phonemes)
- choose a category e.g. animals, countries, boys' names
- work around the group in alphabetical order (*Austria, Belgium, Canada, Denmark, Egypt*).

Letter lists (reinforces initial phonemes)
- as above, but see how many nouns can be thought of for a single letter (*Brian, Basil, Bertie, Bob, Barnaby, Bruce, Ben*).
Let a 'compere'/MC award special bonus points for unusual examples – a gong adds to the fun. Add a twist by using digraphs instead of single letters (*Shirley, Shelley, Sheila, Shona, Sherry*). An alphabet chart may be needed as a prompt for some pupils.

I went to town and saw ... (reinforces rhyme/alliteration)
- beef up the old 'I went to market and I bought' game by giving it a bit of local interest – a local theme park or attraction
- set conditions, e.g. all items must begin with a certain letter/must rhyme
- each pupil in turn repeats the list that has gone before and adds one more (e.g. *'I went to Chessington and I saw: Boyzone, Basil Brush, (Mr) Blobby*).

CLASS/GROUP ACTIVITIES
The class works in teams or groups divided into pairs to provide a competitive element. Any of the circle game ideas above can be adapted for a quick team or group activity as a 'finisher'. These could be extended to a whole class challenge.

How many can you find? (reinforces alliteration)
- the class is asked to produce the longest list of animals/towns etc. beginning with '*B*' (try challenging another class to do better). Be creative with categories - e.g. 'football teams' could include foreign clubs.

Simon says ... (reinforces auditory discrimination)
- choose a particular blend or phoneme (e.g. '*sp*' or '*f*')
- when the teacher says a particular word the pupils have to repeat it if it starts with the chosen sound but they must not say the 'odd sound out' e.g. *Simon says - say spam, say spout, say spot, say shot, say spoil.*

Tongue twisters (reinforces alliteration)
- pupils copy or create their own (the level of support can be controlled e.g. alliterative words provided beforehand and produced by class brainstorming).

'Tell me a sound' (reinforces auditory discrimination)
- class or group sit in a circle
- a leader sits in the middle with a small sponge ball or bean bag
- the leader throws the ball at random to someone in the circle and asks *'Tell me the last sound in...'* giving a word at random (or from a pre-written list)
- if the sound is voiced correctly, the pupil remains in the circle and the game continues. (Try other variations - *the first/middle sound in...*)

Limericks (reinforces rhyme)
- teach pupils the rhyme scheme (a, a, b, b, a)
- try leaving out end rhymes and asking pupils to supply the final words.
  e.g. *There was a young lad from Ipswich*
  Who suffered a terrible ------ (itch)
  He lay on the ground
  And did not make a ------ (sound)
  After rolling all over the ------ (pitch)

Kim's Game (reinforces rhyme)
- place objects which all rhyme or all begin with a certain letter on a tray
- after a minute, these are covered
- pupils must try to remember all the objects.

Feely bags (reinforces auditory discrimination)
- pupils have to describe object hidden in bag to the class/group
- clues regarding first letter, last letter, sounds like ... can be given by arrangement.

SONGS AND RHYMES
'Agga Do' (reinforces rhyme)
- adapt familiar songs and tunes to provide useful practice in rhyme etc.
  agga two, two, two, turn around and touch your ------ (shoe)
  agga three, three, three - if not you it must be ------ (me)
  agga four, four, four - turn around and touch the ------ (door)
  Try adapting current pop songs/football chants of the moment etc.

Raps (reinforces rhymes)
- pupils will probably be able to recommend a few examples
- write them out and let them highlight all the rhyming pairs
- let them learn an example, practise - then have a talent show
- let them teach each other
- try writing a class rap based on a school trip or special event
  (*'Now listen everybody and I'll tell you where we'll be ...*
  At Kentwell Hall - guess what we're gonna see ...')
- compare amount of rhyming pairs with a commercial rap.

'*McDonalds*' (reinforces syllable counting)
- this one, sung to the tune of 'arrum sa, sa' is useful for counting syllables
- once the pattern of syllables in each line is known further variations can be dreamed up
  A pizza hut, a pizza hut (2 x 4 syllables)
  Kentucky fried chicken and a pizza hut (7 + 4 syllables) (repeat)
  McDonald's, McDonald's (2 x 3 syllables)
  Kentucky fried chicken and a pizza hut (7 + 4 syllables) (repeat)
- encourage pupils to think of creative alternatives ('*a Ford Escort, a Ford Escort*' or '*Norwich City, Norwich City*' …).

Old scout/guide songs can also be used successfully.

'*Pick a sound*' challenge (reinforces auditory discrimination)
- pupils are given a margarine tub with the challenge to collect as many items as possible in their tub beginning with the same letter (or digraph etc.)
- they must be able to put the lid on
- encourage them to involve parents
- allow a week and discover the results.

Teaching phonics

The pupil experiencing reading difficulties at Key Stage 2 is likely to have partially acquired some of the requisite skills, but knowledge of the sound/symbol system may be patchy and insufficient to allow steady progress to be made. The value of assessment at this stage will help the teacher identify any strengths in approaches to reading (this will be important to build into any remedial programme) or any weaknesses, which will need supporting. It will be important, for example, to identify which of the 44 phonemes in the English sound system are known (see appendix) and which still remain to be taught. For many pupils, intervention will be necessary to plug gaps in knowledge and to give structured practice and reinforcement in using a range of reading strategies. Sometimes it is necessary to go back to the beginning by assuming no prior knowledge of phonics and to teach the sounds in a structured and carefully graded way. If this is the case, it is likely that the SEN Co-ordinator would also be involved in planning any programme of support. *The National Literacy Strategy* now provides a graded structure (this is summarised in the appendix).

The pattern of spoken English (and its representation in spelling) is a complex one, yet as Davies and Wareing (1995) contend we are putting pupils at a disadvantage if we allow them to believe that one letter of the alphabet always makes one sound (known as OLMOSM, One Letter Makes One Sound Method). Consider the different ways of writing the 'ee' sound:

be	tree	key	seat
chief	seize	centipede	people
magazine	encyclopaedia		party

Children need to be aware of these differences and encouraged to look for analogous spelling patterns in the text. A framework for teaching literacy skills based on the 44 sounds of English has been devised by Davies and Ritchie. The THRASS programme (Teaching Handwriting Reading And Spelling Skills) is now being used in many LEAs and also abroad. It uses a multi-sensory approach and has support activities available on ICT software. This attention to words beginning with the same letters or containing letter strings or the same word in different places complements and reinforces some of the strategies discussed in the previous section on visual approaches to reading. We can see how such strategies are interconnected and mutually supporting. The way in which spoken English is represented in spelling *is* complex, but not too complex that it cannot be taught systematically to young pupils:

> There is overwhelming evidence that an early understanding of sounds (phonemes) and their spellings has a powerful impact on pupils' reading and writing development.
>
> (The National Literacy Project 1997)

The order of teaching phonics

If a pupil is being taken back to the beginning and is being re-taught the sound patterns and print symbols of English, then it will be necessary to consider in which order this should occur. The National Curriculum gives some guidance in its programme of study for English (Key Stage 1) stating that opportunities should be provided for pupils to identify and use a range of letters and sounds including combinations of letters, blends and digraphs. In the past there has been some consensus (Reason & Boote, 1994) about the need to move from initial letter sounds, through consonant digraphs and initial consonant blends through to vowel digraphs, more complex consonant digraphs and trigraphs, then onto silent letters, word endings and polysyllabic words. *The National Literacy Strategy* specifies in detail and sets out an order for the teaching objectives for phonics and vocabulary at 'word level' (see the appendix).

Some pupils at Key Stage 2 may already have a reasonable knowledge of certain phonemes and only need help with particular letter sounds or phonic combinations. If a comprehensive programme of intervention is required, it may be worth looking in more detail at the order of introduction for the initial sounds. The structure set out by Broomfield and Combley (1997) in their helpful book introduces a small number of sounds at a time in a way which allows them to be combined to form rime endings and also reinforces their frequency within early key words. For example, the first four letter sounds to be introduced (*i, t, p, n*) are presented as individual letter sounds and the alphabetic names are also taught. These letters are then used to form the rime endings '*it*', '*ip*' and '*in*' and their use is reinforced in the key words *I*, *it* and *in*.

Some Ideas for Developing Phonic Skills at Key Stage 2

Sounds hunt (reinforces auditory discrimination)
- provide pupils with copies of pieces of text (photocopies, old school letters, comic pages, sections of newsprint etc.)
- give them a highlighter pen
- ask them to find all the words containing specific sounds (blends, digraphs, word endings etc.).

Word searches/acrostics
- teachers and pupils will be very familiar with these. Let pupils write their own (it may be necessary to provide the words or part of the structure)
- when pupils have produced their own examples do use them with other pupils (or make a class puzzle book).
  (Some pupils will not be able to cope with word searches which go from right to left or those which are vertical. They should be provided with left-right words to find.)

Personal dictionaries
- consider having additional pages/sections for particular initial blends/digraphs
- make a class 'rhyme dictionary' (this can be used to assist on writing poetry/raps/ limericks etc.).

Structured reading material
- look out for schemes that have a phonic strand e.g. *Oxford Reading Tree* and *All Aboard* (use selectively as appropriate)
- some schemes are based on phonics e.g. *Fuzz Buzz*. This scheme works well with some pupils (CD-ROM/Language master cards available)
- some schemes which are not 'phonic' as such have additional material which provides practice with phonic exercises/word classification/cloze procedure etc. An example is *Wellington Square* (a CD-ROM is available)
- other publications such as Folens *Foundations* includes a wide range of additional materials for both auditory and visual skills.

Wider reading
- find books and poems that have a strong rhyming element (it can still be fun to do a bit of choral speaking – especially if famous poems are 'rewritten' by the pupils:
The boy stood on the burning deck, his feet were covered with blisters.
He couldn't put his own shoes on and so he wore his sister's etc.).

Card games
- snap, pairs, rummy, pelmanism, lotto can all be based on phonics and provide targeted practice
  (enlist the support of parent helpers in producing such packs of cards)
- if playing 'Bingo' try to add a bit of variety by appointing a caller and thinking up some new 'calls' e.g. *'22 - pass the glue, number 1 - currant bun, 34 - shut that door'* etc.

'Missing sounds'
- simple sentences are provided set out on worksheets
- target words have a key sound omitted (a choice is provided in brackets)
  Manchester United wear a r_d strip (a, u, e)
- try vowels, blends or digraphs etc.

Phonic co-ordinates
- draw a grid – 3 x 3 (larger grids can be used)
- label axes: a, b, c/1, 2, 3
- provide picture clues below for grid references e.g. A1 =
- the CVC word is written in the appropriate square.

Phonic flip-books
- using a slim 'vocabulary notebook' sized book cut this into three sections across the width, without detaching from the binding
- write CVC letters down each page
- pages can then be turned at random to create new words.

Word-slides
- create a workcard giving a list of onsets (single letters, blends or digraphs) down the left-hand side
- on a second piece of card (shaped like a ruler with a slit inserted almost top to bottom) write a rime ending (e.g. -at)
- the card fits over the first piece of card and slides up and down creating new words (e.g. *b-at, ch-at, spl-at* etc.)

'Sound spinners'
- make two hexagonal card spinners in different colours with a spent match or similar through the centre
- write vowels or vowel digraphs ('ee', 'ai' etc.) on one spinner and consonants on the other
- pupils have three spins to create a word (CVC)
- played in pairs, points can be awarded for each 'real' word created.

Word sums
- give pupils multi-syllabic words on card
- let them segment them into syllables
- provide boxes for each syllable within a word (❑ + ❑ + ❑).

Syllable cards
- multi-syllable words are written onto cards
- they are cut into 'syllable' chunks (e.g. *de - part - ment*) for sorting and sequencing.

Syllable pairs
- as above, providing sufficient 'syllables' for a game of pairs to be played
- can be used to focus on particular phonic units (e.g. word endings such as '*ing*').

Plastic/magnetic letter activities
- always useful for creating words and changing key sounds within words.

Football teams
- choose a particular football team whose name reflects a particular sound to be concentrated upon e.g. Ipswi**ch** Town (**ch**) or Lei**c**ester City (soft '**c**')
- pupils try to collect a 'full team' of words containing the appropriate sound (i.e. 11 plus subs).

'The longest word family' list
- choose a phonic unit e.g. 'or' and ask the pupils to find as many words as they can which contain this sound (*or, for, sore, motor, horse, story, score, pore, orchestra, escort, doctor* etc.).
  Make sure that this is an orally based activity or else pupils will give words such as *work, word.*

'Sounds' rummy
- this is played in the traditional way but here based on collecting words containing particular 'sounds' (e.g. '*ow*' - *bow, now, power*)
  Again this must be an oral activity.

'Sounds' pelmanism
- have a set of word cards which feature sub-sets of words containing particular 'phonic groupings' (e.g. '*ing*' - *bring, sling, finger, drinking* or '*ly*' - *slowly, quickly, fondly, happily, coldly*) and play the game in the traditional way.

Word chains
- select a CVC word e.g. '*sap*'
- ask the pupils to find as many words as they can containing these letters
- the letters have to be in the same sequence but can be divided by other letters (e.g. *sap, slap, stamp, slapped, staple, sapling, sample*)
- this can either be an oral or a written exercise.

Multi-sensory teaching

It needs to be remembered that pupils with reading difficulties may be over-relying on one strategy to the exclusion of developing others. They may also have poor auditory or visual memories which makes it difficult for them to retain information, even when it has been taught specifically. Teachers are sometimes at a loss to know how to help pupils who appear to have grasped information one day, but seem to have completely lost it again by the next. Often the best way to support these pupils is to use a multi-sensory approach. This means trying to employ as many of the senses as possible so that the possibilities for internalising and retaining information are maximised. Teachers who employ such methods will be utilising the pupils' strengths by focusing on their preferred strategies, whilst at the same time supporting and developing their weaker skills and allowing them to use and practise these in a structured way. The key feature of multi-sensory teaching is to involve a simultaneous input from visual, oral, auditory, tactile and kinaesthetic channels in the learning task.

SENSORY INPUT	PERCEPTION
Visual	seeing shapes of letters, words and sentences
Auditory	hearing the sounds of letters, words and sentences
Oral	saying letter names or sounds, words or sentences
Tactile	touching/tracing letter shapes, words and sentences
Kinaesthetic	writing letter shapes, words and sentences

(*'ROBAs' Reading Opportunities Based on Assessment*, published by Suffolk LEA, 1996)

Some practical ways of using multi-sensory techniques to develop phonic skills
ICT

Try the SEMERC or REM catalogues which include a range of software from different companies. There is usually an approved service for schools. There are a range of packages and programs available, some with on-screen text accompanied by speech, e.g.

- 'Clicker Plus' (Crick Software)
- 'Speaking Starspell' - draws attention to how words are built (Fisher-Marriott)
- 'Cloze' - a cloze procedure program for PC. Type in your own text and select which words/characters to hide (SEMERC)
- 'An Eye for Spelling' (ESM Software) - shows pupils the correct way to spell words through joined script. Words are built around chosen letter patterns
- 'Learn More About Words' (Inclusive Technology) reinforces reading and spelling - suitable up to Year 4
- 'Wordshark 2' (White Space) - 26 games to reinforce word recognition and spelling
- 'Win Tray' (LETSS) - encourages pupils to predict hidden letters in text, the text is then developed and revealed to the reader
- 'Inclusive Writer' (Widget) - pictorial support to aid spelling, recognition of word families and grammatical structures
- concept keyboard overlays can also be produced to reinforce particular teaching points.

34

Language Master

Cards can be pre-recorded to show and demonstrate onset and rime, syllable segmentation, rhymes etc. Pupils listen to worked examples, read the cards, then copy by recording their own attempt. Headsets can be used to aid concentration.

Taped materials

Programmes such as 'Breaking the Code' and 'Phonic Blending Tapes' (Learning Materials Ltd.) enable pupils to work with headsets at their own pace and level to listen to sound sequences which are identified and ticked off in an accompanying workbook.

Six kits covering CVC words to three syllable words, prefixes and suffixes.

Reading age 5+ (Breaking the Code) 5.5-8 years (Phonic Blending).

Interest age 6-11 years (Breaking the Code) and 6-16 years (Phonic Blending).

3 - Teaching reading through contextual/language strategies

If pupils are going to be able to read interesting reading material they will need to be able to use their learned skills purposefully. Once learner readers have acquired a small store of known sight words and, wherever possible, attained some basic phonic decoding strategies then they will need to combine these skills in order for efficient reading to take place. It is here that reading for meaning, contextual cueing and language strategies come into play. How the adult assists or supports reading is crucial.

Fluency within reading
The fluent reader learns to use the following processes:

- instant recognition of most words
- anticipation of what words will come next
- hypothesising about the correctness of their decision
- discrimination of words that are similar
- rejection of incorrect conjectures
- acceptance of deductions
- confirmation of the choice.

All this is done with speed.

We read to gain information, to be entertained or amused for enjoyment, or to be persuaded. The more we read the better we read and the more we are enabled to gain pleasure or extract ideas. There are two ways of predicting words when reading. One can be through visual generalisations or analogies and the other through substitution through the meaning. Once pupils become more competent at decoding teachers should try to get them to listen to the sense rather than to rely solely on the visual pattern of the letters and then to use controlled guesswork where they are encouraged to look at the parts of the word such as initial letters and make a guess from those. In this way the pupils are given an additional strategy for reading unknown words.

Pupils with reading problems in Key Stage 2 may have a long way to go before they attain competent use of these skills. However, unlike a younger early reader they may already have many skills to draw on. The difference between a reader in Key Stage 1 and a failing reader in the latter stages of Key Stage 2, is experience. Teachers have to keep in mind that by Year 3 pupils who have reading problems have been in school between seven and nine terms. Thus they have been the subject of much teaching of reading and have been involved with many books despite their difficulties to acquire easy access to the written word. By the time they leave Key Stage 2 at the end of Year 6, the gap between their experience of books and their reading attainments may be considerable. Their reading may not be fluent but it contains much that can be worked on and added to. This might still be an onerous process, however.

Children need to learn:
- that reading can be a pleasurable and satisfactory experience
- that reading makes sense
- that books and other texts are a source of enjoyment, information and understanding
- a readiness and acceptance of the need to self-correct errors and to revise their ideas about texts and their contents
- that they can use previous knowledge of other texts, information from the pictures, information provided by the punctuation, ideas about how language operates and their own general knowledge
- that guesswork can be a useful strategy in learning to extend their reading

- to use all strategies and cues automatically in combination so that they can select books suitable to their interests and needs
- to have confidence that they will learn to read
- concentration and persistence.

This might seem a daunting list but with careful planning by the end of Key Stage 2 the majority of the 'failing' readers should be reading more competently. The last two points will be dealt with in the following chapter as this concentrates on the motivational aspects of reading.

Assessment in the areas of language and understanding

In order to provide the necessary help, teachers must know what the pupils can do. Again assessment is so important. The following questions which pertain to how the pupil approaches reading, should be asked:

- what is the reader's general response to the texts including:
  - attitude to reading
  - perseverance
  - level of dependence and independence
  - awareness of own performance
  - level of concentration?
- the reader's present ability to gain meaning from the texts?
- the reader's ability to talk about the story line such as
  - explanation
  - description
  - prediction?
- how well does the reader answer questions from the text and how are these questions interpreted?
- how does the reader actually tackle the text?

(Refer back to the observational checklist in the chapter on assessment for further details.)

As with teaching visual and auditory strategies of reading, when one prepares activities for helping pupils to read contextually teachers need to establish what the pupil can do already and build on this in order to develop the appropriate skills. Therefore, teachers should identify the pupil's most competent strategy and extend this by providing reading passages or reading activities which enable the pupil to practise this skill. Once confidence is high then other strategies can be developed.

Reading is more than merely a decoding exercise

Most teachers will have come into contact with weaker readers who have good oral ability. However, sometimes these pupils do not treat reading as something to which one needs to listen or even as something concerned with the use of words. They do not transfer this knowledge to the reading process. They read as if they are merely undertaking a mechanical exercise. Beyond the acquisition of very basic reading skills, pupils' reading attainments and proficiencies can depend very much upon the amount of reading they are engaged in and their involvement with it.

There are several activities which might promote self-listening and extracting the meaning.

- Give the pupils as much opportunity and encouragement as possible to practise their reading, at whatever level, even if they appear to start with just basic sight recognition or phonic decoding. At times comment upon the text and ask questions or suggest something that is not strictly within the text. The pupils should try to answer or correct the ambiguity.

- Pupils need to believe that texts are meant to be understood and thought about if they are going to understand what they read and cope with comprehension exercises. Therefore, any stories that are read to pupils must be interesting and thought-provoking so that they discover a love of books. Conversations about the books are important.

If pupils have weak verbal abilities, limited receptive language and poor expressive skills it may be more difficult for them to read with meaning, to use contextual skills or to gain meaning from unknown texts. It is always possible that teachers might expect too much too soon, so careful assessment of the pupils' problems is important and the selection of appropriate texts to match reading and language abilities is most significant. Much work should be undertaken on language and vocabulary, and language enrichment opportunities should be provided. The following ideas can be used:

- Spend time on developing expressive language by talking about stories, etc.
- Devise language activities; extend vocabulary by asking and explaining.
- Use pictures for helping to develop knowledge of words.
- Check reading books and match them with the written vocabulary level against the understanding of the pupil so that the pupil gains maximum information and enjoyment from these.
- Share reading and discuss the books.
- Use other supporters as a team of 'language helpers' so that vocabulary enrichment takes place as well as giving time for extended expressive language work.
- Carefully introduce subject-specific vocabulary and model and rehearse language.
- Allow the pupil to practise and rehearse in a 'safe' environment, e.g. in a one-to-one environment or in a small group, so that the pupils feel sufficiently at ease in order to ask whenever a word or concept is not readily understood. This is more likely to occur in a small group situation.
- Devise activities such as repeating sentences and working on oral cloze.

There are times when it is important to teach pupils how to use books as widely as possible. This may come indirectly when the pupil is reading individually from the book or direct instruction may be given to the whole class or to groups. Ideas for this:

- Include the use of the index, the table of contents and how to interpret the 'blurb' on the back of the book. Activities can be provided where pupils are asked to find books with a certain number of chapters or they are asked to decide what might be written about in certain chapters because of the chapter headings. They can also categorise books according to the publishers' information on the back or according to the illustrations on the cover.
- In order to show pupils how important this information is for choosing books devise activities where the pupils write their own tables of contents and summaries of the books' topics.
- If written work is still weak then allow pupils to either dictate to an adult scribe or try using tape-recording/dictaphone facilities.

The importance of using questions to gain meaning from texts
As has been stated, unless reading for meaning occurs when the pupil works with the text then the activity becomes merely one of decoding. Therefore, it is important that pupils answer questions at least orally when they are involved with reading. Conventional comprehension questions are often disliked as the pupils begin to feel that their enjoyment suffers if they have to read and then answer a question. Therefore, some 'games' or activities can be devised out of texts especially written for comprehension purposes. Examples of these are:

- Giving the answers first and then seeing if the pupils can find out what the question may have been. This turns the pupil into the teacher.
- Devising different types of questions. The easiest are those that are literal as the answers are given within the text.
- Other questions can be predictive where the pupils give their own ideas.
- Questions can also be implicit and, therefore, have to be explained.
- Many pupils find it hard to give their own opinions because they feel that there is a 'right' or a 'wrong' answer. It is important that they learn to express opinions and to give reasons. Black and white pictures can be used initially where the pupil is asked to express opinions about the colours of objects and to justify why they give particular responses.
- To extend study skills and help the pupils to read swiftly, the text can be given and the adult can ask a question. The pupils have to scan through to find the answer rather than reading all the text. The pupils have to recall one or two keywords which makes it easier for them to find the answers.

It is as important for pupils to learn to ask questions as it is for them to be able to respond to questions. Here the teacher has to try to encourage pupils to go beyond reading and to think about the ideas raised, the story-line or the particular information given and also to query what they have read. The following suggestions might be helpful:

- Choose a passage from a book, a chapter or a story, and copy onto an overhead transparency. Show the title first and ask the pupils to predict what the rest of the text might be about.
- Reveal the first sentence and discuss what is known about the story so far.
- Encourage the pupils to ask questions. The teacher should only answer using the information provided so far. The answers the teacher is able to give are 'I don't know' or 'It doesn't say'.
- Questions that the pupil ask should be those concerned with prediction such as 'Do you think?' and then the teacher can state what he or she actually thinks.
- Show the next sentence and the same format continues until the end of the passage.
- At the very end the whole story is read and discussed.
- It can be useful if a chart can be drawn up which reminds the pupils about how to ask questions.
  FACT: Who? What? Where? When?
  INQUIRY: Why? Do you think?
  VOCABULARY: What does ... mean?
  EXPERIENCE: Have you ever?

The importance of selecting appropriate books
If pupils are going to achieve they should be given texts that they can read orally with 90 per cent to 95 per cent accuracy. If this happens then teachers know that the books they are providing are suitable for pupils to work with on contextual strategies. If the texts are at an appropriate level of difficulty the pupils can be encouraged to take time to study any unknown words and then reread the entire sentence or phrase in which they appeared. They should not find too many of these within each sentence otherwise fluency will be compromised. Repeated readings of text are found to produce a marked improvement in word recognition, fluency and comprehension. (See the text level work in *The National Literacy Strategy*.) Both fiction and non-fiction books can be chosen.

Pupils with reading problems may need to read widely at a similar readability level because of their lack of confidence. Reading the same books will help to develop their confidence. They should be able to read these as often as they need, as it is most likely that they will become either bored with the current book or confident enough to go on to something else after a few attempts. The following points might be helpful in this respect:

- Encourage pupils to have both a familiar book (as this will help confidence building) and a 'new' book for learning purposes. If the pupils are totally accurate and fluent after two to three rereadings then this might be the time to encourage the pupil to go on to the next book.
- Provide a 'selected' choice of books at the same level in order to develop independent reading. A balance needs to be achieved as 'favourite' books and texts are always desirable but pupils need to extend their skills. If the pupils are particularly reluctant to change their books then a structured and supported reading environment will be necessary such as shared reading and group reading situations (see later). The reading expectations can be gradually extended in small steps. The 'failing' reader should not be overwhelmed.

Sometimes if pupils feel that the books they are given to read are too difficult they try to work out their own practical solutions to overcome this perceived problem. Often they try speeding up and reading on, glossing over the harder words, in order to reach words which make sense. The result is a string of words rather than meaningful sentences. Sometimes they try to get the general idea of the text rather than to strive for accuracy. So that pupils do not become discouraged teachers might:

- Praise this effort and show the pupils how their attempts matched the sense but not the exact words. Encourage rereading (perhaps a small section of the text), this time looking at each word, especially the difficult ones.
- Pupils who 'make up the text' might not realise that they have misread because they are learning to listen to the sense. An adult is needed here to help and support until they are confident at coping with these techniques themselves.
- Some weak readers often tend to over-rely on context and meaning which can make it difficult for the teacher to decide when it is necessary to either encourage or restrict this method. It is easier for the developing readers to understand the text and to deal with unknown words through contextual clueing if they are fluent at word recognition.
- When confronted by unknown words, encourage pupils to complete the whole sentence before coming back to the unknown word. It is then helpful for the pupil to reread the whole sentence so this is placed within a meaningful context.

Encouraging reading as a language activity
Modelling as a means of improving reading is a helpful way of encouraging weaker readers to hear the language of books at a more difficult level than they would be able to read for themselves. Pupils will benefit from hearing a fluent reader, a teacher, parent or other adult, acting as a model. This particularly develops an appreciation of syntax (knowledge of the construction of language, grammar, within the English language). It is important that pupils are encouraged to follow the words so that they can match the shapes of the words visually whenever possible with the sounds. Often pupils enjoy story tapes and there are also speaking stories on computers which can become models. Reading to pupils is also very important and this is a factor that should be stressed where partnership with parents is concerned. Even older pupils enjoy listening to stories, especially those that they want to be able to read but are as yet unable to. Pupils with reading problems at Key Stage 2 often have ambitions to read popular authors such as Roald Dahl or C. S. Lewis and feel that they are 'readers' once they have mastered books such as these. It can also help to give pupils the chance to be the expert by encouraging them to read to younger pupils. In this way they become the 'model' for others and are helped to see its relevance.

Reading for pleasure can also be used to encourage reading and this can be acquired in various ways such as:

- Pupils should read for ease and enjoyment by attempting non-book materials.
- Simple magazine articles can be short, interesting and informative.

- Comics can provide a way into reading even though the language and the grammatical structure may not be of the highest quality.
- Easy and well-loved books often provide great pleasure.
- A range of more demanding materials such as plays, poetry, short stories, biographies, autobiographies and non-fiction materials should be provided.
- Reading for information surrounds pupils in their daily lives such as letters, lists, instructions, football programmes, TV listings and information books and all these have a place in reading for meaning.
- Devise activities to encourage pupils to read these materials (e.g. give them some written instructions to follow, write them a letter).
- It can also be beneficial for pupils to have their day's work written for them in the form of a list on the board rather than having these given orally.

Sharing texts with adult supporters

The importance of pupils reading with and to supportive adults cannot be too greatly emphasised. The terms 'paired', 'shared' and 'collaborative' reading approaches have been in use for many years and employ slightly different techniques. These approaches are often used for enabling readers with problems to extend their reading strategies.

Any 'shared' approach means that there must be partnership. In order to set this up there should be the choice of fiction and non-fiction books and it might be sensible if adult and pupil make choices alternatively. If the pupil always chooses independently the book might not provide the text necessary for language and contextual strategies to be worked on. If the school has a system of graded books then use books other than the core scheme, leaving the latter for the teaching of more discrete skills. Although books can be quite expensive it is important that there is a wide range of books within the school or class library. Prior to embarking on any shared reading approach one needs to determine certain prerequisites:

- The level of ease or difficulty of the book to be read. Knowing the readability of books written for core reading or supplementary reading schemes is easy. Publishers indicate this in their literature and there are books like NASEN'S *A-Z* which give much helpful advice about both readability levels and interest levels. It is more difficult with fiction and non-fiction books. However, it is important that the books chosen for any shared reading approach are neither too difficult nor too easy. For this type of reading to work best then the books should be at 'instructional' level. Readability methods have been referred to earlier.
- The length of time and frequency needed for the pupil to engage with the text. Some years ago it seemed to be the practice that the busy primary class teacher was able to listen to two pupils reading one or two pages of their reading books simultaneously. This occurred because it was felt that pupils had to be heard every day and that there was only the class teacher to do this. Now it is accepted that it is more important that the reader reads all the book or as much as can be achieved in at least 5 to 10 minutes. Where sharing reading is concerned at least 10 to 15 minutes is needed especially because of the preliminary discussion and questions that need to be posed. The pupil needs to know what is expected and this should be consistent.
- The suitability of the place where reading is to take place. This needs to be conducive for reading and, therefore, should be quiet and comfortable and away from obvious distractions. This can cause a problem in a busy school. Some classes have a 'reading corner' with comfortable chairs which forms a quiet area. Sometimes these are partitioned slightly by book cases and cupboards to make it easier for concentration. Some schools have other quiet areas which can be used. Comfort and quietness are necessary. Adults prefer to read in this type of situation although they can usually cope with reading on busy trains and buses. Pupils with reading problems need distractions minimised.

Once a suitable environment has been arranged the adult, whether this is the class teacher, learning support assistant or other adult, has to follow certain ways of working. In order to encourage the pupil to be interested in the text the supporter has to show interest in it. A good choice of book is necessary in order to get the pupil to maintain curiosity about what happens within the story etc. If the pupil is not apparently interested in any of the books then the adult supporter sharing the reading might have to work quite hard to make the books interesting and worthwhile reading. It is important that the pupil has a good relationship with the adult so that trust is built up and if this happens then the pupil may want to read something the adult says will be a 'good' story.

Preliminary discussion about the book should focus on the probable contents from the cover, the title and the pictures etc. As new pictures are seen they need to be discussed and questions should be asked about pages read so far. If there is vocabulary which seems to be difficult then this needs to be explained. However, it should not just be the adult who talks but the pupil should be encouraged to ask questions and to lead the discussion. However, care should be taken to achieve a balance between time spent on oral language activities and the main aim of involving the pupil with reading the text and building up strategies within reading.

It is important that the adult, where this is not the class teacher, is given information about the particular type of support the 'paired' or 'shared' reading requires. The supporter must know, therefore, how to cope with any errors or misreading. The adult who shares reading with the pupil should be aware of how to enable the pupil to try an unknown word or how to supply the unknown words after about 5 seconds of the pupil being silent or struggling with decoding. The technique of 'Pause, Prompt and Praise' can be used. A summary of this approach can be found on page 21 of *Teachers and Parents Together for Reading* (Shirley, Smith & Visser, 1996). Briefly adults listen to the pupil reading and give verbal praise for sentences read correctly, self-corrections after errors and when words are read correctly after prompting. When the pupil halts time should be given to see if the word is known or worked out and then prompts should be given to aid the pupil to cope with the problem word. The supporter must know whether words supplied by the reader that are contextually correct but visually incorrect should be corrected. Often it is appropriate to make a note of the substitution and then praise at the end of the reading when the actual word can be looked at. (There is a piece of recorded shared reading in the appendix.) An important part of the role of the supporter is that any praise that is given is both justified and genuine. Nothing is worse than insincerity and pupils are quick to pick up on platitudes.

The 'rules' for the reading session must be understood by both parties. It is here that the different procedures and techniques need to be set out. Paired reading involving a pupil and an adult (rather than a peer) can comprise slightly different procedures than those for other sharing methods. Both readers, supporter and pupil, may read together word by word keeping a steady pace – being not too fast and not too slow. If the pupil is following without reading then the reading should flow and appear lively rather than jerky or flat. This can be difficult when the natural rhythm of reading is delivered at the pace of normal speech and the pupil cannot follow at that speed. However, if the adult tracks the text by pointing to the words or the lines then the pupil can 'see' and 'hear' how the language of the text runs along. A non-fiction book can be read in a slower, more deliberate manner because of the information it is delivering.

In some paired reading procedures, a signal is given such as a tap on the table to signify that the pupil wants to take over all the reading but so often this seems contrived rather than natural and it often breaks the flow of reading. If such a procedure is worked out then the supporter has to cope with becoming quiet straight away and the pupil praised for independent reading. Whereas when reading was simultaneous and the adult pointed to the words and lines it may be easier for the pupil to carry out this tracking process. However, sometimes the adult may need to continue in order to help the pupil read with some fluency. The supporter needs to be aware when to join back in and a signal might be needed to indicate when the pupil wants a rest.

For many adults it is easier to divide the session into sections covering the preliminary language activities, then the sharing of the text, the pupil's turn and the final oral language and feed-back session. Any direct teaching of skills which have been noted during the session can follow on from this.

It is important to record comments when a pupil is learning to read or to extend reading strategies as these can be most helpful. These form part of ongoing assessment activities. Comments made should be both positive and helpful in informing further programmes. The pupil should be given feed-back and should also be able to give his or her own comments.

Guessing at unknown words sometimes makes pupils feel that they do not have to strive for accuracy. Learning necessitates taking risks. However, if the adult attempts to correct every error then the reader will become discouraged. The following suggestions may be helpful:

- Disregard some errors. Usually it does not matter if the reader fails to get all words exactly correct all of the time. Provided what they are reading makes sense, then the context will make it clear if an error changes meaning.
- Continue to encourage the pupils to listen to themselves as they read.
- Do not discourage guessing and do not insist on the reader reading too carefully so that slow stilted reading occurs. This can become disheartening for both the listener and the learner.
- Do not correct errors too quickly or the learner will not come to understand that reading is an activity in which sense plays a large part.

Guided reading

This term appears in *The National Literacy Strategy* and is used for the time when the teacher can teach reading (and writing) to at least one ability group per day for a sustained period of time. Guided reading is described as a 'counterpart' to shared reading. The difference between the two strategies is that whereas shared reading involves a supporter, usually an adult, reading with the pupil and modelling and teaching the skills and processes involved, guided reading focuses on independence in reading. Guided reading within the Literacy Hour takes the place of an individualised reading session as it is a group activity which has been carefully structured. Because of this it should increase the time given for sustained reading. The process involves:

- grouping pupils in ability groups of about four to six
- selecting texts which match the readability levels of the pupils (graded texts, from reading schemes or from supplementary readers as the pupils' reading attainments improve)
- supplying each pupil with an individual copy
- the teacher introducing the text and familiarising the pupils with the storyline etc.
- the teacher pointing out keywords that need to be known
- pupils reading the text independently with the teacher assessing and supporting pupils individually
- as pupils progress with reading skills, silent reading should be encouraged with questions being asked to assess what has been read
- the teacher monitoring and noting problems etc. so that the text level objectives within the Literacy Hour framework are met.

Guided reading as a group reading activity is dependent upon pupils reading within the same readability band and being reasonably fluent within this. Often pupils with reading difficulties find it hard to either read with others, to read independently to others or to listen to others reading. Group dynamics will be important as will detailed knowledge about individuals' reading attainments, abilities and self-esteem.

Extending reading and providing other activities

As pupils become more proficient at reading, teachers need to devise extension reading activities which will encourage the pupils to listen to the text in a meaningful way. Retelling stories after hearing the story read aloud is a useful way of making sure pupils listen to the text. This can occur either as an individual activity or in pairs or groups. The story or particular chapter is read out loud to pupils and they can follow if they wish (this should be encouraged wherever possible). If this is recorded on tape, or is on a computer that speaks as the text is shown, then the pupils can follow the text or refer back to any part that they might have missed or need to have reinforced. Writing activities can be given in order to find out what the pupils have learnt from the text. Ideas to help here are:

- The pupils can read silently or in their groups or pairs. Sometimes adult support may be needed. When they feel happy with the text they then retell it in their own words.
- Pupils can either write individually, in pairs or collaboratively in a group depending upon age and ability.
- Sometimes it is helpful to use a tape-recorder or adult for scribe.
- Skeleton story outlines which give connectives can be given to help the retelling. For example, phrases such as 'one day', 'then', 'after that', 'later', 'lastly' can trigger the pupils to write parts of the story in sequence.
- Boxed outlines or spider diagrams also help retelling. (There are many books which explain these, e.g. *Learning to Learn* by Malone & Smith, 1996.)
- For those pupils who have particularly poor writing abilities, give them the actual text cut into sections so that they can read these and sequence them correctly.
- Fairy stories can be used for retelling with different characters or with different endings. Books such as Ahlberg's *Jolly Postman* can be the focus of this type of work where particular letters are read, the actual tale is read for comparison and another letter or story is made up. Key Stage 2 pupils will cope with Key Stage 1 texts if they understand that these are being used for a particular purpose.
- Other ideas such as 'brainstorming' (listening and recalling as much of the text as is possible), recalling events in sequences (sometimes using ready-prepared cards with main events written on them) and predicting using the pictures in the books are also useful.
- Constructing continuous stories is a useful and interesting way of making reading seem real to pupils. The pupils dictate the sentences after discussion about the content of the stories and the arrival at a title. The book is word processed. The pupils practise the passages until they are fluent and they practise the important and difficult words. This continuous story unfolds week by week and holds the interest well.
- Foster their enthusiasm for books by encouraging them to respond to texts in different ways such as by writing (the most difficult), drama, painting or drawing.
- Books are not just for reading. They can also be written and illustrated and then shared either with their peers or with younger pupils. Thus reading each other's writing such as publishing books and newspapers or magazines can be seen as an important part of reading texts.
- Letter writing can provide interesting and meaningful reading. Corresponding with pupils in other areas of the country or the world might be set up.
- 'Urgent' (transactional) and necessary reading such as notes, labels, lists, instructions, post-its and letters should form part of the reading programme.

Using cloze procedure to help reading

Cloze procedure involves using a passage of text which contains spaces where the missing words have to be supplied by the pupil. Reading as a cloze procedure activity helps both syntactic and semantic knowledge. It is usual to use prepared passages where every tenth word is missing. In this way both high interest and function words are missing and at times words will be omitted from the beginnings of sentences. It is not usual to give pupils who have problems passages with more than one in every seventh word missing as this makes it too difficult for choosing words. There are points that can be made about this activity:

- If pupils are unused to this procedure within reading then it may be easiest for them to have the last word in each sentence omitted as this is the easiest way of supplying unknown words.
- At times this can be changed to multiple choice activities.
- Cloze passages can be made with different words omitted such as all adjectives, adverbs, conjunctions or verbs as well as regular lengths between each gap. These can enable pupils to understand syntactical structure.
- Sometimes if parts from a reading book are given as cloze passages then the pupils could either try to produce words that are the same as the author or words that can be different from the author. They can try to 'beat the author' by producing more appropriate or interesting words.
- Cloze procedure work should not always be done as an individual activity but as collaborative exercises as well.
- Cloze procedure activities can enable pupils to read without them realising that they are involved with reading because they feel they are working out exercises.

The use of non-fiction texts when helping pupils to read contextually
Although many pupils want to read non-fiction books these can be more difficult than conventional reading books. Frequently pupils attempting non-fiction texts need much support from adults. Often keypoints are not emphasised and the sentences, paragraphs and sections are placed arbitrarily rather than logically (following a structured sequence). Therefore, details do not follow in a predictable way. Here teachers might help in the following ways:

- By explaining the specialist vocabulary and working with the pupils on the language as these often can seem quite demanding. At times the specialist language is poorly supported by explanations.
- By encouraging and helping the pupil to follow the text when reading. Information books often contain too many ideas or concepts per page and each page has a slightly different type of layout.
- By helping the pupil to use the illustrations. Sometimes these neither reinforce nor complement the text and, therefore, distract and confuse the reader.

Organisational implications
There are many organisational implications for teachers in order to set up specialised or extra help for pupils with reading problems who do not fit easily into established reading groups or who need extra work to that given in the Literacy Hours. These pupils need sympathetic handling. Their enjoyment of the reading process may have to be rekindled. Books may need to be chosen for their particular approach to text so that the pupils work from the known in a meaningful way and, therefore, build on their current attainments and strategies. It is so important to create and use a reading environment which provides time and opportunities for fostering the whole reading experiences of the individual pupil. The later section on organisation within the classroom will go into this area in more detail.

4 - The motivational aspect

There are two types of poorly motivated or reluctant reader and both pose separate problems to the class teacher when trying to foster and generate enjoyment of reading and also trying to develop their reading attainments. One is the reader who actually can read but for some reason does not want to read and who avoids reading wherever possible. Sometimes these readers will not read fiction but will read information and non-fiction texts or comics and magazines. The other is the pupil who has difficulties with reading and, therefore, because of this does not want to risk further failure and becomes indifferent to reading, judging it 'boring' rather than 'hard'. Pupils can start to become demotivated in Key Stage 1 and so by Key Stage 2 are particularly hard to teach and cause problems both in school and at home. If difficulties persist then it becomes harder to foster their self-esteem.

One of the most important factors in helping pupils in Key Stage 2 to become more competent readers is increasing their motivation or the building up of their self-esteem as readers. If pupils have lost faith in themselves because they struggle with texts then they might give up trying. Reading must be made a successful and pleasurable experience for them wherever possible. If successful reading occurs and is improved through continued reading teachers need to foster pupils' motivation to practise what (to them) is a difficult activity.

It is particularly important to help pupils who have continuing and seemingly deep-seated reading problems not to give up when faced with the many reading tasks that are part of the Key Stage 2 curriculum. Often these pupils are not fluent at their measured readability level so reading is slow and stilted. As reading becomes more challenging they often give up all together. It is important that their reading problems are not emphasised within the classroom as pupils do not want their peers to know about their difficulties. There are several strategies which teachers can use once the pupils' reading levels have been assessed. If the pupil is 'fluent' at a low reading level then:

- Work on this for a while so that the pupil gains confidence from quite easy texts.
- The pupil's own dictated words could be taken (in story form wherever possible) and word-processed for reading and rereading. A reward system could be provided for accurate reading and as the pupil becomes more proficient more difficult words (either sight words or decodable words) could be added from time to time. In this way the pupils monitor their own reading and become aware of progress.
- The techniques of using shared reading and paired reading with an adult have already been described in the previous chapter and these are very important for reluctant readers as are listening to story tapes or using ICT. Even though pupils need not read along with the text they are able to hear and see familiar words and stories.
- Reading must be made as manageable as possible even if this is done in very small steps.
- The provision of very simple texts for pupils to read to younger pupils at school can be a successful way of raising self-esteem.
- The setting and negotiation of achievable targets can help to encourage the pupil to self-monitor and, therefore, to see progress.

Developing a reward system

Because struggling readers often do not read regularly it is difficult to motivate them and make them aware that reading might be an enjoyable activity. Sometimes the use of a reward system or the giving of praise by another adult is a helpful teaching strategy. Year 3 pupils may react favourably to star charts and stickers whereas the older pupil might need some other kind of tangible reward. Teachers must know their pupils' preferences. Pupils need to feel that they are making some headway with reading texts even though they are at a very low stage of reading. The following techniques have been successfully used in various schools:

- A points system can be developed in class. All pupils and in particular those pupils with problems can earn points by reading at home and at school. Different amounts of reading for different readers will 'earn' different points. These targets should be challenging as pupils will not accept praise or rewards for something they feel they have not 'earned'. There will need to be an end reward after a certain number of points have been achieved. Depending upon the pupil there can either be a chart for all to see displayed within the reading area or the pupil can have a personal chart which is shared only with the teacher and the home.
- Sometimes praise from the headteacher is a reward in itself as are stickers or some other types of visual commendation. It is probable that the struggling readers will not want their efforts praised in front of others in an assembly but some schools have award 'certificates' for successful achievements and here the reluctant reader might receive a certificate for reading a certain number of books.
- Those classes which use Circle Time techniques can reward reluctant readers when either their peers or adults notice their recently acquired reading attainments and remark on these. (See the references for details of Circle Time publications.)

The provision of suitable reading material

Teachers need to find some method in order to 'switch on' non-motivated readers to the enjoyment of reading if these pupils also have reading difficulties. Published reading materials often fail to hold interest especially if the pupils feel that the content of the stories are not at their interest level. Teachers need to try to provide high interest materials with a lower reading ability level as it is particularly demotivating for the older reader to be given what appear to be books used for younger pupils and which might have been on offer in Key Stage 1. Unfortunately this occurs because the Key Stage 1 texts are at the readability level of the older pupil. Therefore, wherever possible:

- Texts should be of a high quality and as attractive as possible.
- Teacher-made material should be well written and attractively presented if it is to be acceptable.
- The pupils should have the use of ICT as multi-media packages can be both motivating and stimulating, as can any ways into reading which take away the difficulty of the pupil coping with the written print on paper.
- The provision of non-fiction books could be offered as an alternative.

Encouraging the unmotivated more able reader

It is not only the weaker reader who stops reading books. There are also fluent readers who appear unmotivated towards reading fiction for pleasure. Frequently these are boys who do not have role models where reading is concerned or who prefer to be active rather than what is felt to be passive when involved with a book. They will often read magazines but not books and both teachers and parents seek guidance in how to extend their reading. The following points may be helpful:

- If boys want to read about football then football stories should be found if possible or football information books. Sometimes teachers write these themselves. (This refers to any type of interest the pupil might have but there are some interests which seem to be written about more than others.) They should also be encouraged to read newspaper articles or magazines which can be enlarged on the photocopier to ease reading.
- After the pupil has read these books, information books on other subjects should be tried and if any other areas seem to interest them stories on those subjects should be provided wherever possible.

- It may be possible to interest the reader in books which are recommended by other pupils of the same age.
- There are often magazines or articles which review books, tapes and videos for the pre-teen to teenage age group. It is important that teachers are able to keep up to date with the new fiction that is written each year and the particular books that are written for pupils with reading problems.

Pupils with specific learning difficulties

Some weak readers appear to be verbally able. Their language usage is very good and they can respond to questions about books read to them. However, because of their reading problems they have little interest in reading and it is often difficult for teachers to help them understand their problems and to come to terms with them. Many such pupils are those who may be dyslexic and have specific reading difficulties. These problems should be discussed with the pupils. This book is not the place to go into specific learning difficulties but it is recognised that it is quite important for dyslexic pupils to know that their reading problems are not of their own making but also it is important for them not to hide behind their problems. They, in fact, have to work harder than others and it is most important that teachers understand their difficulties and give as much help and support as possible.

Reading a range of books

A recurring problem experienced by teachers in Key Stage 2 is that they find it hard to motivate their pupils to read a range of books. The reading scheme book is read and sometimes this takes a considerable time to get through. Non-motivated children need regular reading practice which is well monitored and this is not always easy for the class teacher to organise. The following ideas might be helpful:

- One should make sure that there is a range of fiction and non-fiction books at particular readability levels.
- A 'Books I Have Read' notebook can be provided for recording those chosen and in order to make sure that books have been read, each book should be checked by hearing at least three pages read out loud with a signature from an adult. (It is not always necessary to hear every word on every page of every book, especially if these books are being read for enjoyment rather than for purposes of direct instruction.) A reward can be given for every 'x' number (to be determined for each individual pupil) of books read.
- There could be a particular author chosen for the week and everyone has to have read something by him or her or have acquired some information about the author.
- Suitable class and group readers should be provided so that reading can also be collaborative. This is explained more fully by *The National Literacy Strategy*.
- Reading must become high profile in those classes where there are reluctant readers. The use of videos of famous stories, the sharing of 'best' books and a wall display of recommendations may tempt the demotivated reader to try a book.
- Pupils should be encouraged to talk about their best books with time allowed for this.
- Pupils can be presented with a negotiated 'challenge' such as book passports which are stamped on completion. These 'book challenges' can be 'themed'(e.g. a specific author, a particular genre, different subject areas such as sea or sport etc.).
- Tallies or charts are kept and praise or incentives given for successful completion.
- Other teachers can be asked to give praise but, as has been stated previously, praise must be seen to be genuine.
- Adults from the community may volunteer to share their reading interests with the pupils. If 'local heroes' (such as football players) visit to read with pupils and to talk about the books they read when at school, reading becomes high profile.

Supporting reading

As it is not always easy for the class teacher to give well-monitored and regular practice to those pupils who lack motivation, other supporters can help as:

- Parent or other adult helpers and support assistants can be deployed to hear reluctant readers. Teachers must make sure, however, that these supporters know how to listen and how to help.
- Older primary pupils (those in Years 5 or 6) can be used but only if the younger (Year 3 or Year 4 pupil) can cope with this. This situation needs careful handling as some pupils may feel foolish reading with their peers.
- If there are secondary school pupils who can give some time for listening to readers this can be an invaluable asset.
- Daily quiet reading times should be organised (outside the Literacy Hour) but teachers will have to make sure these pupils are actually reading and this is not always an easy task.
- A routine for extra reading should be established which would have to be seen as a bonus not as a punishment.
- Home reading should also be encouraged.

Another problem encountered by teachers dealing with pupils with low motivation and poor self-esteem is that they often read with no expression and in a low quiet voice in order to make sure no-one can hear their errors. It would be good to raise their confidence by helping them to read with expression and the following suggestions might be helpful:

- The reading materials must be within their capabilities and it would be helpful if the pupils can hold sentences in their heads. If that is not a problem they can learn some sentences or poems which can be recited rather than read. This helps to stop word-by-word decoding.
- Books should be chosen with both dialogue and questions in them so that the voice can naturally rise and fall.
- If similar work is taped the pupil can listen to how one reads with expression.
- Simple playlets where dialogue is essential can be useful. There are quite a lot of acting situations which can encourage expressive and dramatic reading. Here the use of the tape recorder can be helpful because pupils can listen to good and bad examples and can record their own.
- Working with puppets or cartoon characters helps the shyer pupil by placing the focus of attention on the puppet.
- Pupils can also record and write their own scripts and can act out comic strips or poems.
- The pupils could be encouraged to 'read' stories to younger pupils where they have to use other voices to keep the pupils' attention.
- Pupils learn from modelling, by example. When reading to their classes, teachers should, at times, be over-expressive (or under-expressive) to prove a point.
- In order to help the pupils' flow of reading they should be allowed to read at an easier level of reading but the pupil should be aware why this is being done.

Gaining from the text

In order to find out what the pupils have gained from the text and how they respond to the text, teachers need to employ more strategies than merely asking questions. Pupils who find reading difficult and who labour through the texts often have the end of the activity as their goal. This is usually the end of the book or the completion of a certain number of pages. There are a range of activities which can be provided to help the pupils think about the text rather than making them feel that they have to just read the words. Some of these include:

- Listing and discussing events and characters in the book that are liked and disliked.
- Pupils could pretend that they are reporters and they have to interview the main character. This can be done either as a written or an oral exercise.
- Some written exercises could include writing a letter to the main character which could either give or ask for advice, writing a newspaper story about one of the incidents in the book, or writing a radio or TV report about one of the incidents.
- As an alternative to writing, tape-record some of these activities.
- A non-writing activity could be based on drawing an advert for a book or making a game based on a book.
- Similar activities can be devised for instructional texts or information books.
- Pupils can make up their own questions about texts for others (or the class teacher) to answer. In this way they have to read the text without realising that this was a reading activity.

Confidence comes through getting things right. Pupils' confidence in reading will grow if they feel they are reading correctly so rereading of familiar texts should be acceptable. The goal is to help the pupils feel that reading is pleasurable and that despite their problems they will try texts that are difficult and challenging and that they will enjoy and read with confidence. Teachers will see how successful they have been when the pupils ask to read, when they voluntarily pick up a book and read, when they ask for books for rewards at school and at home as presents, and when they say that they enjoy reading and enjoy books. They will have their favourite authors and will grow up to become readers.

PART 3
Organisation in the classroom/resources/working with parents and other adults

Organisation

Dombey (1992) said 'Organisation can make or break the teaching of reading.' This statement seems even more pertinent since the introduction of *The National Literacy Strategy* and teachers having to organise the Literacy Hour.

The Literacy Hour is divided into four parts:

- 15 minutes shared text work
- 15 minutes focused word/sentence work
- 20 minutes independent work
- 10 minutes plenary.

It is the 20 minutes of group and independent work where word and sentence level work takes place which will need most of the teacher's organisational skills. They should work with at least one ability group each day which indicates that most pupils will have to become independent workers. Therefore, work that the pupils are given needs to be meaningful and achievable. It is expected that there should also be other opportunities in the day for extra reading activities.

When planning reading activities the following organisational factors will need to be considered:

- *one to one teaching.* This may need to be included.
- *group teaching.* Decisions about the organisation of groups within the class might be based on attainment or ability. (This has implications for the dyslexic pupil who might be a very weak reader but who might have quite high cognitive abilities.)
- *use of learning support assistants*
- *use of other adult helpers*
- *peer pairs* (either the same age or a different age)
- *home/school arrangements.*

Individual teaching may not be easy to arrange during the Literacy Hour. Nor may it be easy to arrange during the rest of the week. Individual work is necessary for careful assessment and is a requirement of *The National Literacy Strategy*. Most pupils appreciate the individual attention that reading with their teacher provides and often a programme of work based on the pupil's particular needs can only be given on a one-to-one basis. Instead of the focus being to hear the pupil read, the individual session then becomes a reading conference where assessment, teaching and learning can take place (see appendix).

Group work provides opportunities for pupils to learn from each other in a supportive way. During group work pupils can have conversations and discussions about texts which will give them more opportunities for speaking and listening. Practice with turn taking provides opportunities for learning by peer modelling. This also encourages them to try out and rehearse strategies in a less threatening setting. Paired or group activities at word level work will also help those pupils who are weaker at reading.

It is important to guard against using group work as a time-filling activity without proper attention given to the learning outcomes set for the pupils. Teachers must ensure that all pupils are actively and purposefully engaged and do not let others in the group do the work for them.

Teachers need to decide which approach they are going to use with their slower and weaker readers. A variety of reading systems have been designed to help the slower readers in primary schools. An evaluation of 20 different approaches to the teaching of reading, *What Works for Slow*

Readers? The Effectiveness of Early Intervention Schemes by Brooks et al. (1998), categorises the approaches into those which focus on 'phonological skills', 'comprehension skills', 'self-esteem' and on the use of 'ICT'. Partnership approaches are also reviewed in some depth. Their findings with reference to pupils at Key Stage 2 suggest that 'in general, normal schooling does not enable slow readers to catch up'. Pupils with reading difficulties will, therefore, need to be given extra support and teaching if they are to progress. The conclusions reinforced the point that phonological skills are an integral part of the reading process. Comprehension skills were found to improve if these were directly targeted and ICT approaches would only show results if they were 'precisely targeted'. Putting a pupil with a computer without adult support often fails to maximise learning outcomes. Partnership approaches were found to be effective as long as those who took part as the reading partners were given appropriate training which has implications for home-school programmes, adults listening to reading and peer approaches. Also it was found that pupils' reading will improve if their low self-esteem is targeted. This publication could be used by schools and LEAs to determine the most appropriate way of allocating resources for the teaching of reading, especially if one of the large-scale programmes is used, for although seemingly expensive the report concludes that they 'can give good value for money'.

There may be difficulties organising classrooms. Pupils will have to learn how to become independent learners. They will have to learn not to interrupt the teacher when he or she is working with a particular group. Thus there will be the need for alternative resources. Encouraging independence of working should take the same format throughout the school so that pupils will not have to learn a new set of working habits from class to class. Group dynamics will have to be looked into carefully. The quiet pupil must not be overlooked. It may be necessary to provide some individual places for those pupils who distract others. Some schools provide work stations within the classroom or find other areas in the school that can be used. The use of other adults will become very important and schools will have to decide when the Literacy Hour is to take place as all teachers will be able to find uses for classroom support assistants. Schools with learning support teachers will have to decide when individual or small groups get supported. It will have to be decided which part of the Literacy Hour can be left or what other lessons can be missed without loss.

Resources

It may be that about one-fifth of 7-year-olds have difficulty with reading and thus they fail to gain the expected target of Level 2 in reading in the Key Stage 1 assessments. Many of these pupils have made a start with reading and will need extra help in order to catch up. Others will have made little headway with the complex process of reading. Reading schemes to help in the reading process have been considered earlier in this book.

The use of non-fiction texts can bring problems although more reluctant readers may find these more pleasurable and acceptable than story books. These problems need to be noted:

- Key points are not always emphasised and are often embedded within the text.
- Sentences and sections are not always logically set out on the page and are, therefore, difficult to follow.
- Details do not always follow in a predictable way especially if there are diagrams or illustrations which break up the text.
- There is often too much use of specialist language without sufficient support or explanations.
- The illustrations and diagrams do not always reinforce or complement the text.
- The pages contain crowded information with too many ideas and concepts.
- Sometimes the index or content pages are inadequate.
- The layout makes the text difficult to follow.
- Although written for a certain age group the readability is too advanced.

ICT has been mentioned as being helpful for pupils. As with any reading schemes or allied teaching materials computer programs should provide real learning experiences. They should be able to be worked on by individuals and they should record what has been achieved so that adults can monitor this. There may be some pupils who have very deeply entrenched reading problems which are particularly hard to shift and who have otherwise average to above average cognitive abilities. In the secondary sector these pupils may need alternatives to reading and writing such as voice activated computers. However, it is necessary to try to enable such pupils to be as literate as possible before they leave the primary sector.

Working with parents and other adults

An HMI report (Autumn 1990) confirmed other findings that 'the quality and extent of parents' support for pupils' reading had a positive effect on their standards of reading.' Reading has to be part of the parent/teacher partnership and, therefore, parents need to understand the reading process and the school's reading policy. The majority of parents want to help their children. Those who appear reluctant may feel intimidated by the task or even have literacy problems themselves.

It may be easier for parents to read to younger children, to those who are preschool or in Key Stage 1. By the time their children are in Key Stage 2 and 'failing' they may not want to be read to any more, they may refuse to bring their reading books home to practise and they might find that younger siblings are overtaking them, thereby making matters worse. Parents need help if these attitudes are seen at home. They need to understand that reading is not just reading books and that magazines, comics and football programmes are acceptable especially if these spark off an interest in words. Parents need to know what kinds of books to buy their reluctant readers and how to help them make choices about suitable reading material. Parents should be helped not to take the blame for their children's reading problems.

Schools should be open and honest about pupils' problems. Parents need to be kept informed about difficulties and they also need to be told about any progress made. Parents' views should also be asked for.

In order to involve parents of Key Stage 2 pupils in reading activities with their children, the following suggestions could be followed:

- Allow parents access to book areas at the end of the school day (daily or weekly) in order to browse and select books with their children.
- Use every opportunity such as parents' meetings, open days or parent assemblies to discuss books and show some of the 'best' books for different age groups and interests. Use the schools' library service if possible.
- Display new books centrally before these go to individual classrooms and allow parents and their pupils to look at them.
- Use one prominent noticeboard in the entrance hall, if possible, as a 'book board'. Display information about books. Encourage pupils to find reviews about their favourite books. Supply post-its so that parents can write up the names of books, authors and publishers that they either bought or borrowed that were successful with their children.
- Encourage two-way dialogue in reading logs. Do not always insist that the pupil has to read the school book but encourage recording the reading of their own books or library books. Ask the parents to be as truthful as possible about how their children reacted to certain books. Give them guidance about how they can comment by providing examples. Do not insist that a book has to be read at home if the pupil really dislikes it.
- Encourage reluctant readers and their parents to participate in the annual Book Week. Change the theme of this each year and organise a competition where all pupils can take part (such as dressing up as a particular book character, drawing posters for favourite books or even writing to authors, with parental help).

53

- Set up book clubs which are attractive for all readers.
- Let parents know what is the 'set text' for the week's Literacy Hour. Weaker or reluctant readers could work on posters which could be placed in a central area so that parents are kept informed.
- Organise parental workshops to share with parents how to listen to their children reading using methods such as 'Pause, Prompt and Praise' or paired reading.
- Explain about teachers listening to pupils reading in school, the value of the longer reading conference and the problems with hearing reading in short bursts.
- Give them tips about listening to their children at home which would include items such as:
  - make reading pleasurable
  - try to read without distractions (younger siblings, the TV)
  - be interested in the chosen book
  - talk about the pictures, the characters, the plot
  - be positive and praise rather than say 'no' to incorrectly read words
  - supply unknown words (unless the teacher has given particular strategies to be followed)
  - let children read and reread if that is what they want to do
  - do not mention that you feel a book is too easy or too difficult (but you may have to help more with the latter)
  - read to yourself so that your child sees that you feel reading is enjoyable.

Parents can become helpers within the classroom as can other adults. They can listen to individual readers and play word games with groups. They can support pupils using a computer and can help with the Language Master or story tapes. However, whatever these adults do they will need some advice and training in what they are doing and why they are doing it.

Most schools have learning support assistants although in some schools fewer work in the Key Stage 2 classes as they are often employed within Key Stage 1. These extra adults will be crucial to the work achieved with slower and reluctant readers because they are part of the school and are known by the pupils as helpers. With the Literacy Hour and at other times of the day the pupil with reading problems can have extra individual attention and help. Again it is necessary for the adults to have some training on the reading process so that they can make the most of the individual sessions. There may be allocated learning support assistant time or even teaching time for pupils with a Statement of Special Educational Needs. Again this needs to be built into the class organisation.

Conclusion

When *The National Literacy Strategy* was first published there was little reference to pupils with special educational needs. Later additional guidance was sent to schools. This included a section on 'children with special educational needs'. The needs of two broad groups of pupils were addressed. The first, the larger group, includes those whose levels of literacy attainment are below those expected for their ages and whose problems can usually be overcome within the normal school teaching strategies. The second is a much smaller group containing pupils with severe and complex learning difficulties who will need different teaching strategies.

The suggestions given within this additional guidance are general in nature, covering differentiation of work, the use of extra support and of pupils working both within and outside the class during the Literacy Hour, termed 'parallel sessions'. It is noted that within the group and independent work sessions of the hour individual needs can be met because the work set for different groups can be differentiated. It is also pointed out that pupils with specific learning difficulties should not always be put into the lowest ability group because of their good conceptual knowledge. Objectives from the Literacy Hour can be broken down into smaller steps for individual pupils' needs and written on their IEPs and the importance of ongoing assessment and evaluation is emphasised.

It is hoped that *Key Stage 2: Helping with Reading Difficulties* has provided ideas for the management and teaching of pupils who have reading problems. Intervention strategies will be required if pupils are to make up ground. Such intervention needs to be based on a thorough and comprehensive assessment of the pupil and should employ a multi-sensory approach which covers a range of strategies and techniques so that strengths can be developed and weaknesses underpinned.

Appendix

Precision Testing: Probe Sheet

Name: ....

Skill to be improved: ....

Date started: ....Daily for 1 minute

Words I can read in 1 minute:

Days	1.	2.	3.	4.	5.

My record was: ....

Appendix

Precision Testing: Probe Sheet

Name: ....

Skill to be improved: to read topic words on Egypt

Date started: ....Daily for 1 minute

Words I can read in 1 minute:

Days	1.	2.	3.	4.	5.

My record was: ....

Egypt	tomb	mummy	pyramids	Egyptians
pyramids	mummy	Egypt	Egyptians	tomb
Egyptians	pyramids	tomb	mummy	Egypt
mummy	Egypt	Egyptians	tomb	pyramids
pyramids	mummy	Egypt	Egyptians	tomb
mummy	tomb	Egypt	pyramids	Egyptians
Egypt	tomb	mummy	pyramids	Egyptians
pyramids	mummy	Egypt	Egyptians	tomb
Egyptians	pyramids	tomb	mummy	Egypt
tomb	Egyptians	pyramids	Egypt	mummy

Checking passages for word types

LEE WORKS FOR MORE MONEY (a chapter from an unpublished set of easy to read stories for Key Stage 2 pupils)

'Lee wants more money so he goes to his mum. "Can I do some work for you?" Mum gets him to wash up. Lee doesn't like this but he works hard. He gets £2 a week for this. But Lee wants more money so he goes to his dad. "Can I do some work for you?" Dad gets him to dig in the garden. Lee doesn't like this but he works hard. He gets £2-50 a week for this. Soon Lee has got his money for another fishing rod.'

keywords	phonic 1	phonic 2	other
wants	mum		wash
more	gets		
so	Lee		
he	dad		
to	week		
his	soon		
can	fishing		
I	rod		
do			
some			
for			
you			
money*			
goes			
work*			
him			
to			
up			
doesn't*			
like			
this			
but			
dig			
in			
garden*			
has			
got			
another			

This example shows that most of the keywords are 'list 1 high frequency words' to be taught through sight recognition through Year R to Year 2 (with those starred for Key Stage 2) according to *The National Literacy Strategy*. The phonic words show sounds to be taught through Year R to Year 2 . There is only one irregular word indicating that this passage should be in the reading capabilities of pupils having coped with the reading at Key Stage 1.

THE CIRCUS (part of a chapter from an unpublished set of more difficult stories written for Key Stage 2 pupils)

'*The pupils clattered excitedly into the classroom. Their voices were loud and Mrs Simpson had to shout quite firmly to make herself heard. "Quieten down, class 6," she said. "It's register time." It took some minutes for the chattering to stop.*

After the register Mrs Simpson asked her class what all the fuss was about. "It's the circus, miss," answered Paul. "There's a competition for all pupils. If any of us wins first prize in either the story writing or the painting all the class can go to the circus free. The circus will be here in three weeks' time." Mrs Simpson knew that she would have to let her class enter for the competition. "All right," she said, "but first it's spellings." There was a loud groan from everyone.'

keywords	phonic 1	phonic 2	other
the	clattered	excitedly	Mrs
pupils*	classroom	quieten	minutes
into	voices	register	answered
the	loud	circus	either
their	Simpson	competition	
were	shout		
and	quite		
had	firmly		
to	class		
make	chattering		
herself	stop		
heard*	fuss		
down	miss		
she	Paul		
said	wins		
its	first		
time	prize		
it	story		
took	writing		
some	painting		
for	free		
after	weeks		
asked*	let		
her	enter		
what	spellings		
all	groan		
about			
there's			
all			
if			
any*			
of			

keywords	phonic 1	phonic 2	other
us			
in			
or			
can			
go			
will			
be			
here			
three			
knew*			
that			
would			
have			
all			
right*			
but			
first			
from			
everyone*			

Despite this passage containing more words than the first example the majority of the words are 'list 1 high frequency words' to be taught through sight recognition through Year R to Year 2 (with those starred for Key Stage 2) according to *The National Literacy Strategy*. The phonic words show sounds to be taught through Year R to Year 2. This passage would probably be at an instructional level for pupils with reading problems in Key Stage 2 as long as they have covered and retained most of the prescribed work specified for Key Stage 1.

Recorded shared reading

THE CIRCUS (part of a chapter from an unpublished set of more difficult stories written for Key Stage 2 pupils)

'The pupils clattered excitedly into the classroom. Their voices were loud and Mrs Simpson had to shout quite firmly to make herself heard. "Quieten down, class 6," she said. "It's register time." It took some minutes for the chattering to stop.

After the register Mrs Simpson asked her class what all the fuss was about. "It's the circus, miss," answered Paul. "There's a competition for all pupils. If any of us wins first prize in either the story writing or the painting all the class can go to the circus free. The circus will be here in three weeks' time." Mrs Simpson knew that she would have to let her class enter for the competition. "All right," she said, "but first it's spellings." There was a loud groan from everyone.'

The pupil reading this was a Year 5 boy, Harry, with a learning support assistant supporting him. His attempts are in bold with the following code for the supporter.

* PrPh = prompting through phonics/syllabication
* PrM = prompting through meaning/reading on
* PrR = prompting through rereading
* T = told.

The pupils clattered (**excitedly** PrPh) into the classroom. Their voices were loud and Mrs (**Simpson** PrPh) had to shout quite (**firmly** PrPh) to make herself heard. (**Quieten** PrM/R/T) down, class 6 she said. It's (**register** PrM) time. It took some minutes for the chattering to stop.

After the register Mrs Simpson asked her class what all the fuss was about. It's the circus, miss (**answered** PrM) Paul. There's a (**competition** PrPh) for all pupils. If any of us wins first prize in (**either** T) the story writing or the painting all the class can go to the circus free. The circus will be here in three weeks' time. Mrs Simpson knew that she would have to let her class enter for the competition. All right, she said, but first it's spellings. There was a loud (**groan** PrPh) from everyone.

Out of 130 words Harry read all but eight (about 94 per cent) showing that this was at independent level. He was told only two words and coped with the others on the second attempt. The learning support assistant made a note of the unknown words and chose the following phonic patterns for further work: 'ir' and 'oa'. Harry was encouraged to reread the passages to his mother at home so that he could show his fluency.

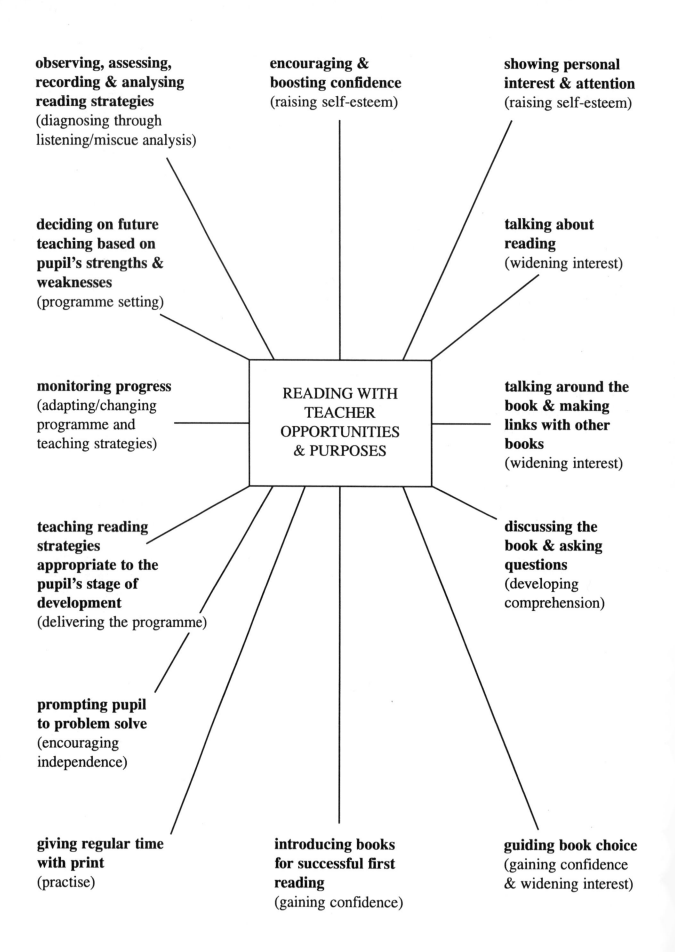

observing, assessing, recording & analysing reading strategies (diagnosing through listening/miscue analysis)

encouraging & boosting confidence (raising self-esteem)

showing personal interest & attention (raising self-esteem)

deciding on future teaching based on pupil's strengths & weaknesses (programme setting)

talking about reading (widening interest)

monitoring progress (adapting/changing programme and teaching strategies)

READING WITH TEACHER OPPORTUNITIES & PURPOSES

talking around the book & making links with other books (widening interest)

teaching reading strategies appropriate to the pupil's stage of development (delivering the programme)

discussing the book & asking questions (developing comprehension)

prompting pupil to problem solve (encouraging independence)

giving regular time with print (practise)

introducing books for successful first reading (gaining confidence)

guiding book choice (gaining confidence & widening interest)

Adapted from Wendy Bloom: "Has Your Teacher Heard You Read Today?" *Language & Learning* (June 1996)

The National Literacy Strategy (DfEE 1998)

(summary of the specific phonics work to be covered in Years R-2)

Reception	consonant and short vowel sounds a-z, ch, sh, th all letter names
Year 1 Term 1	revise above/short vowel sounds as middle sounds in simple words
Year 1 Term 2	revise above, ck, ff, ll, ss, ng initial consonant clusters: bl, br, cl, cr, dr, dw, fl, fr, gl, gr, pl, pr, sc, scr, sk, sl, sm, sn, sp, spl, spr, squ, st, str, sw, tr, thr, shr common end clusters: ld, nd, lk, nk, sk, lp, mp, sp, ct ft, lt, nt, pt, st, xt, lf, nch, lth
Year 1 Term 3	long vowel phonemes: ee, ea, ai, a-e, ay, ie, i-e, igh, y, oa, o-e, ow, oo, u-e, ew, ue
Year 2 Term 1	vowel phonemes: oo (short), ar, oy, ow, ou
Year 2 Term 2	**air**: air, are, ere, ear **or**: or, oor, aw, au, ore **er**: er, ir, ur
Year 2 Term 3	ear/ea (hear/bread)

The 44 sounds (phonemes) of English

'*a*' as in **a**xe or **a**nd	'*ay*' as in spr**ay** or l**a**te	'*air*' as in p**air** or fl**are**	'*ar*' as in b**ar**
'*b*' as in **b**at or bu**bb**le	'*c*' as in **k**ing, **c**up or **ch**ristmas	'*ch*' as in **ch**ip or di**tch**	'*d*' as in **d**ig or pa**dd**le
'*e*' as in **e**gg or tr**ea**d	'*ee*' as in h**e** or gr**ee**n	'*ear*' as in n**ear** or b**eer**	'*er*' as in t**er**m, sk**ir**t or c**ur**b
'*f*' as in **ph**otograph or **f**ly	'*g*' as in wa**gg**le or **g**ap	'*h*' as in **h**elp	'*I*' as in wh**i**te, m**i**ne, m**igh**t or sp**y**
'*i*' as in b**i**t or t**i**cket	'*j*' as in **j**elly, we**dge** or **g**esture	'*l*' as in **l**ad or ti**ll**	'*m*' as in **m**ug, su**mm**er or co**mb**
'*n*' as in **n**est or **kn**ock	'*ng*' as in si**ng** or wi**n**k	'*o*' as in d**o**g or sw**a**p	'*o*' as in r**o**pe, b**o**ne or c**oa**t
'*oy*' as in s**oi**l or R**oy**	'*oo*' as in h**oo**k or f**u**ll	'*oo*' as in sp**oo**n, gr**ew** or bl**ue**	'*oor*' as in m**oor**
'*or*' as in c**or**k, h**a**ll or s**au**cer	'*ow*' as in n**ow** or m**ou**se	'*p*' as in **p**arty or a**pp**le	'*r*' as in **r**obin, so**rr**y or **wr**ite
'*s*' as in **s**ip, **c**eiling or gla**ss**	'*s*' as in mea**s**ure	'*sh*' as in **sh**op or **Ch**arlotte	'*t*' as in **t**able or ba**tt**er
'*th*' as in **th**ud	'*th*' as in wea**th**er	'*u*' as in disc**u**s, teach**er**, cobr**a** or doct**or**	'*u*' as in f**u**ss or l**o**ve
'*v*' as in **v**iolet or cur**ve**	'*w*' as in **w**ig, **wh**en or q**u**een	'*y*' as in **y**ellow	'*z*' as in **z**ipper, free**ze** or whi**zz**

References

Brooks, G. et al. (1998) *What Works for Slow Readers? The Effectiveness of Early Intervention Schemes,* NFER: Slough.

Broomfield, H. & Combley, M. (1997) *Overcoming Dyslexia: a practical handbook for the classroom,* Whurr Publishers: London.

Bryant, P. E. & Bradley, L. (1985) *Children's Reading Problems,* Basil Blackwell: Oxford.

Curry, M. & Bromfield, C. (1994) *Personal and Social Education for Primary Schools through Circle-time,* NASEN: Tamworth.

Davies, A. & Wareing, S. (1995) 'Graphemic Awareness: The Missing Link', in *Special Children* 1995 issue 87.

DfE (1994) *Code of Practice on the Identification and Assessment of Special Educational Needs.*

DfE (1995) *English - in the National Curriculum,* HMSO.

DfEE (1997) *The National Literacy Project - Framework for teaching* (draft).

DfEE (1998) *The National Literacy Strategy.*

Devereux, K. & Van Oosteroom, J. (1992) *Rebus Glossary,* LDA.

Dombey, H. (1992) *Words & Worlds,* The National Association of Teachers of English (NATE).

Goswami, U. (1995) 'The Role of Analogies in Reading Development' in Gains, C. & Wray, D. eds., *Reading Issues and Directions,* NASEN: Tamworth.

Goswami, U. & Bryant, P. E. (1990) *Phonological Skills and Learning to Read,* Lawrence Erlbaum Associates: Hove.

Hinson, M. & Gains, C. (1997) *The NASEN A-Z: A Graded List of Reading Books,* NASEN: Tamworth.

Hinson, M. & Smith, P. (1997) *Phonics and Phonic Resources - New Edition,* NASEN: Tamworth.

Irlen, H. (1991) *Reading by the Colors,* Avery Publications: New York.

Jaeger Adams, M. (1990) *Beginning to Read: Thinking and Learning About Print,* MIT Press.

Layton, L., Deeny, K. & Upton, G. (1997) *Sound Practice - Phonological Awareness in the Classroom,* David Fulton: London.

Lloyd, K. quoted by Haigh G. in 'Easy Reader', *TES Primary Update* 11.10.96.

Malone, G. & Smith, D. (1996) *Learning to Learn,* NASEN: Tamworth.

McNicholas, J. & McEntee, J. (1991) *Games to Improve Reading Levels,* NASEN: Tamworth.

Moran, H., Smith, K., Meads, J. & Beck, M. (1996) Let's try that word again in a new way! Helping failing readers to learn high frequency words in *British Journal of Special Education* Vol. 23. No. 4 December 1996.

Mosley, J. (1996) *Quality Circles,* LDA: Cambridge.

Moyle, D. (1970) *Breakthrough to Literacy,* Longman: Harlow.

Muggeridge, J. & Bowen, P. (1993) *Sandwell Group Phonic Test,* NASEN: Tamworth.

Reading Schemes The NASEN Guide on CD-ROM (1998) NASEN: Tamworth.

Reason, R. & Boote, R. (1994) *Helping Children with Reading and Spelling,* Routledge: London.

'ROBAs' Reading Opportunities Based on Assessment (1996) Suffolk LEA.

Shirley, J., Smith, D. & Visser, J. (1996) *Teachers and Parents Together for Reading,* NASEN: Tamworth.

THRASS (UK) Ltd., (1998) *Teaching Handwriting Reading and Spelling Skills,* Chester.

UK Reading Recovery National Network *Book Bands for Guided Reading: organising KS1 texts for the Literacy Hour.*

Vincent, D. & de la Mare, M. (1992) *The Individual Reading Analysis,* NFER-Nelson: Windsor.

Useful addresses

Widgit Software Ltd.
102 Radford Road
Leamington Spa
CV31 1LF
01926 885303
Website http://www.widgit.com/

Granada Learning - SEMERC
Granada Television
Quay Street
Manchester
M60 9EA
0161 8272927
Website http://www.semerc.com

REM
Great Western House
Langport
Somerset
TA10 9YU
01458 254700
Website http://www.r-e-m.co.uk